THE SERMONS OF

ST. FRANCIS DE SALES

FOR

ADVENT AND CHRISTMAS

St. Francis de Sales
1567-1622
Bishop, Founder of the Visitation,
and Doctor of the Church

THE SERMONS OF
ST. FRANCIS DE SALES
FOR
ADVENT
AND
CHRISTMAS

Volume IV in the Series

Translated by Nuns of the Visitation

Edited by Father Lewis S. Fiorelli, O.S.F.S.

*"Urged solely by His immense goodness, God
became incarnate for us."*
—St. Francis de Sales

TAN BOOKS AND PUBLISHERS, INC.
Rockford, Illinois 61105

Nihil Obstat: Rev. Msgr. John H. Dewson
                 Censor Librorum

Imprimatur: ☩ Most Rev. Robert E. Mulvee
                 Bishop of Wilmington
                 Wilmington, Delaware
                 August 21, 1987
                 Birthday of St. Francis de Sales

Library of Congress Catalog Card No. 87-50748

ISBN: 0-89555-261-2

Further volumes in preparation.

Printed and bound in the United States of America.

TAN BOOKS AND PUBLISHERS, INC.
P.O. Box 424
Rockford, Illinois 61105

1987

"Let us come close to the crib. If you
love riches, you will find the gold that the kings brought;
if you are looking for the smoke of honors,
you will find that in the incense;
and if you take delight in the delicacies of the senses,
you will find the delicate perfume of myrrh that pervades the stable.
Be rich in love for this adorable Saviour,
respectful in the familiarity
with which you relate to Him,
and delight in the joy of experiencing in your soul
so many inspirations and affections
because you belong exclusively to Him."

—*St. Francis de Sales*

The Sermons of St. Francis de Sales

Volume I   On Prayer
Volume II   On Our Lady
Volume III   For Lent
Volume IV   For Advent and Christmas

TABLE OF CONTENTS

About St. Francis de Sales...........................xiii

Preface...xvii

Translator's Note.....................................xxi

1. Saint John the Baptist Sends His Disciples to Jesus
    Sermon for the Second Sunday of Advent, December 6,
    1620, concerning why St. John sent his disciples to ask
    Jesus if He were the Messias although he already knew
    He was, three reasons why God asks questions, John's
    desire to make Jesus known to the whole world, to
    guide his disciples directly to Jesus and to detach his
    disciples from himself, how St. John adapted himself to
    his disciples' weakness, how St. Paul adapted his
    instruction to his hearers, how Our Lord identified
    Himself by pointing to His works, the spiritual
    significance of these works: the blind see, the lame
    walk, lepers are cured, the deaf hear, dead men are
    resuscitated and the poor have the Gospel preached to
    them, the "scandal" of the Cross and its necessity for
    salvation, Our Lord's praise of St. John the Baptist and
    the reasons He did not deliver it in the presence of
    John's disciples, St. John's unshakable spiritual stability
    and our fickleness, and St. Ambrose's great meekness
    yet unshakable firmness.............................1

2. The Great Humility of Saint John the Baptist
    Sermon for the Third Sunday of Advent, December 13,
    1620, concerning pride and ambition as the most
    powerful temptations, the excellent humility of St. John
    the Baptist in renouncing the most dangerous and subtle
    temptation to pride and ambition, his immediate and
    succinct denial that he was the Messias, the desire of

angels and of all men (even pagans) for the Incarnation, our foolish and untruthful acceptance of honors, St. John's humility in skillfully denying even the honored status that rightly belonged to him—without, however, being untruthful; how we should not excuse ourselves of the very faults we accuse ourselves of but confess them straightforwardly, humility's excellence, affinity with charity, and necessity in order to escape the devil's snares; St. John's lowly description of himself and Our Lord's praise of him, God's perennial humbling of the proud and favoring of the humble, and how all should imitate St. John the Baptist......................20

3. Penitence
   Sermon for the Fourth Sunday of Advent, December 20, 1620, concerning St. John the Baptist as the voice of Our Lord and his obligation to proclaim His word, the corresponding obligation of hearers to listen to and profit by God's word, procrastination and spiritual avarice as reasons why we fail to profit from God's word, two meanings of Isaias' words: Because your malice and wickedness have reached their height, your sins shall be forgiven; the very surprising ways of God's mercy, how cooperation with a grace brings subsequent graces, the Incarnation's occurrence at the height of men's wickedness, God's forgiveness of St. Paul and David and others at the height of their malice, the penitence indicated by St. John's exhortations to prepare the way of the Lord: tempering fear with confidence, getting rid of presumption and pride, straightening our intentions, seeking opportunities for penitence and acquiring an even disposition by mortifying our passions, inclinations and aversions, thus evening out the way for our Saviour's coming...............................35

4. The Coming of the Divine Infant
   Sermon for Christmas Eve, December 24, 1613, concerning vigils, the manna in the desert, the mystery of the Incarnation, Our Lady as Star of the Sea and Morning Star and how she produced Our Lord

virginally as stars produce light, the three tastes of the
manna—flour, honey and oil—and what they represent in
the Divine Infant: His divine nature, His soul and His
body; the shepherds and whom they represent, Our
Lord's swaddling clothes—why He was wrapped in them
and what they teach us, how we should visit and bring
a gift to the Divine Infant, the special individual
consolation each visitor will receive in return, how our
senses and interior faculties are restless and dissipated
until they have chosen Our Lord for their king, and
how we should always remain near Our Lord........50

5. Mystical Aspects of the Mystery of Christmas
   Outline for a sermon for the "Vigil of the Nativity of
   Our Lord, 1614, for the Congregation of the Oblates of
   the Visitation," concerning the Saviour as the
   "Expectation of Nations," Our Lord's two natures:
   human and divine; the mystery of fruitful virginity, the
   four kinds of people according to their attitude toward
   the newborn Divine Infant, the Holy Family as a
   religious congregation and how they practiced chastity,
   obedience and extreme poverty, and the various offices
   of Jesus, Mary and Joseph within this community.... 63

6. The Union of the Divine and Human Natures in Our Lord
   Sermon for Christmas Eve, December 24, 1620,
   concerning the Incarnation as the work of all three
   Persons of the most Holy Trinity, the union of the
   divine and human natures in Our Lord, the three
   "substances" in Our Lord—Divinity, body and soul—
   symbolized by the three tastes of manna: honey, oil and
   bread; how man was made God and God was made
   man in the Incarnation, man as a union of body and
   soul, images of the union of the humanity and Divinity
   of Our Lord: iron inflamed with fire, the fleece of
   Gedeon, a sponge in a vast sea; the reason for the
   Incarnation: to teach us to live according to reason, as
   Our Lord practiced material and spiritual sobriety by
   depriving Himself of all agreeable things, doing God's
   will in all things—and how God does the will of those

who do His; Our Lord's choice of a life of pains and
labors although He could have redeemed us by a single
loving sigh; desire for spiritual consolation vs. humility
and resignation to God's will, and the hidden
profundities of the Mystery of the Incarnation........67

7. The Incarnation
     Sermon for Christmas Midnight Mass, December 25,
     1622, concerning the great Christian feasts and their
     observance in the early Church, the Incarnation as
     God's end in creating the world, the two births of the
     Word: eternal and temporal, the two natures of the
     Word made flesh, and the Eternal Father's goodness to
     us in making His Son a member of our human race. 82

8. Spiritual Circumcision and the Sacred Name of Jesus
     Sermon for the Feast of the Circumcision of Our Lord,
     January 1, 1622, concerning Christian feast days,
     circumcision in the Old Law, Our Lord's Circumcision,
     the spiritual circumcision of the part of ourselves most
     affected by sin, complete spiritual circumcision vs. that
     which is only partial or a mere incision, observance of
     the entire Law of God as necessary for salvation, the
     greater obligation of priests, bishops and religious to
     practice complete spiritual circumcision, the never-ending
     struggle in this life against unruly passions and
     emotions, our inculpability in feeling spontaneous unruly
     emotions vs. culpability in those voluntarily encouraged
     or expressed in words, how it is far better to be
     "circumcised" by another than by oneself, the rape of
     Dina and the willing submission to circumcision by the
     people of Sichem, the fittingness of Our Lord's
     reception of the name of Jesus ("Saviour") on the day
     of His Circumcision, His three essential titles, Jephte
     and the password "Scibboleth," and the sacred name
     "Jesus" as our password for entering Heaven........87

9. The Wedding Feast of Cana
     Sermon for the Second Sunday after the Epiphany,
     January 17, 1621, concerning Our Lord's miracle at the

wedding feast of Cana as the first sign He performed
to manifest His glory, mystical correspondences between
the works of Our Lord, His changing of water into
wine at the beginning of His ministry and of wine into
Blood at its end, the attendance of Our Lord and His
Mother at the wedding feast of Cana, Our Lady's way
of addressing her Son regarding the shortage of wine,
how we should make the proper intentions in our
prayers, the error of praying for the feelings of the
virtues rather than for the virtues themselves, the true
meaning of Our Lord's seemingly harsh response to His
Mother, Our Lady's confidence that He would grant a
favorable response, the way in which Our Lord
advanced His "hour" in response to Our Lady's prayer,
the Holy Eucharist, and how we should follow Our
Lady's advice to do whatever her Son tells us—by
faithfully fulfilling the duties of today so that He may
change the tepid water of our repentance into the wine
of divine love.................................... 103

Index 119

ABOUT ST. FRANCIS DE SALES

St. Francis de Sales, the holy bishop, founder, and Doctor of the Church, is known throughout the Church for his great sanctity, learning, theological knowledge, gentleness, and understanding of the human soul. Through these gifts he converted and guided innumerable souls to God during his own lifetime, and re-converted 70,000 from Calvinism. He continues to direct many souls through his spiritual writings and published sermons. Today St. Francis de Sales is known as one of the great figures of the Catholic Counter-Reformation and of the 17th-century rebirth of Catholic mystical life.

St. Francis was born in 1567 in the castle belonging to the de Sales family in Thorens, Savoy, located in what is now southeastern France. His mother, Francoise, was only 14 years old when Francis, her firstborn, came into the world. This maternity was a dangerous one, the labor was long and difficult, and it was marvelled that both mother and child did not die. It is most noteworthy that a month before the birth Francoise had consecrated her unborn child to Our Lord in the presence of the Holy Shroud, which at that time was kept in the Sainte Chapelle in Chambery, France.

Later, Francis was to have a great devotion to the Holy Shroud because his mother had been delivered much better than expected through her veneration of this holy relic. He considered the Shroud to be his country's shield and greatest relic. It was his favorite devotional picture, and he had numerous images of it painted, engraved and embroidered, placing them in his room, chapel, oratory, study, reception rooms and breviary. St. Francis de Sales wrote that his devotion to the Holy Shroud was due to the fact that "my mother, when I was still in her womb, dedicated me to Our Lord before this holy banner of salvation."

As he grew older, St. Francis de Sales studied literature, law, philosophy and theology in Paris and Padua. Upon finishing his studies, he received a doctorate in civil and canon law. Though he could have had a brilliant secular career, he set his soul on following the call of God to the priesthood, and was ordained in 1593 at age 26. He was consecrated Bishop of Geneva at age 35, and was to remain Bishop of Geneva for the remaining 20 years of his life. Some years after St. Francis de Sales took charge of Geneva, King Henry IV suggested to him the possibility of a transfer to a diocese with more worldly advantages; the saint replied in words that soon became famous all over Paris: "Sire, I have married a poor wife and I cannot desert her for a richer one."

Shortly after becoming a bishop, St. Francis met St. Jane Frances de Chantal, a widow; between these two saints there grew a deep spiritual friendship. St. Francis became the spiritual director of Jane Frances, and with her, he founded in 1610 the religious order of nuns known as the Order of the Visitation, or the Visitandines.

Both of these saints loved the Heart of Jesus, and conceived this Heart as the particular treasure confided to the nuns of the Visitation. It is most remarkable that 60 years before the great revelations of the Sacred Heart of Jesus to the Visitandine St. Margaret Mary Alacoque (1673-1675), St. Francis de Sales and St. Jane Frances de Chantal had very often spoken to their spiritual daughters of this sacred love. St. Francis de Sales stated that the Visitandines who followed the Rule would receive the privilege of bearing the title, "Daughters of the Sacred Heart of Jesus." Although devotion to the Heart of Jesus was at this time very little known, God was drawing these two souls to prepare the Visitation as a holy sanctuary to receive the famous revelations to come. Years later, with His revelations to St. Margaret Mary at the Visitation of Paray-le-Monial, God called this order to share with the entire Church the knowledge of the love of His Divine Heart.

In these Advent and Christmas sermons St. Francis de Sales deems it very important to help his hearers understand the holy mystery of the Incarnation. He himself had once received wonderful supernatural lights on this mystery on the occasion of receiving Holy Communion from Pope Clement VIII on March 25, 1599. Of this experience he wrote, "The day of the Annunciation, having received Holy Communion from the hands of the supreme pontiff, my soul was very much consoled interiorly. God deigned to grant me a great understanding of the mystery of the Incarnation. He gave me to understand how in an inexplicable manner the Word had voluntarily taken flesh through the power of the Father and the operation of the Holy Spirit in the most chaste womb of Mary and so commenced to live among us. The God-Man also gave me a deep and exquisite knowledge of transubstantiation and about His entrance into my soul; He also gave me special lights about the ministry of the pastors of the Church."

St. Francis was also deeply devoted to St. John the Baptist, who is often spoken of in these sermons; he called him the father and the son of the Visitation of Mary. As Providence would have it, he preached his first public sermon on the feast of St. John the Baptist, June 24, 1593—making a deep impression on all, especially his bishop, who was filled with joy at the great graces he foresaw would come to souls through the new "apostle."

As a spiritual director, St. Francis de Sales was for a time the confessor of Blessed Marie of the Incarnation (Madame Barbe Acarie). This saintly woman was a wife, mother of six children, Parisian hostess, mystic, and foundress of five Carmelite convents.

St. Francis de Sales wrote two of the greatest Catholic masterpieces on the spiritual life: the *Introduction to the Devout Life* and *Treatise on the Love of God*. The former shows how holiness is possible for all people in the state of grace, including people living in the world. This book was a best-seller in the 17th century and is still popular today. The *Treatise on the Love of God* covers all aspects of the virtue of charity, the supernatural love of God. St. Francis de Sales' pamphlets against the Calvinist heresy have been gathered together into a book and given the title *Controversies*. The arguments presented in the *Controversies* are just as unanswerable today as when they were written. A statement in this material supporting papal infallibility was studied by the Council Fathers at Vatican Council I in 1870, over 270 years after St. Francis wrote it. Because of his writings, St. Francis de Sales has become the patron of writers and journalists; he has also been designated patron saint of the Catholic press.

Two months before his death, St. Francis de Sales received a heavenly warning of his approaching end. In his will he wrote, "I order that at my burial thirteen candles be lit around my coffin, without any other shield except that of the name of Jesus, to show that with all my heart I embrace the faith preached by the apostles."

At Christmas Midnight Mass in 1622 St. Francis de Sales preached the sermon which was to be his last published sermon. (Sermon 7 of this volume.) His words that night possessed a supernatural eloquence, and afterwards the Mother Superior asked him if he had received some extraordinary grace during the Mass; she said, "It seemed to me that I saw the Archangel Gabriel by your side as you were intoning the *Gloria in Excelsis*." The saint answered somewhat vaguely, but when pressed further, replied, "It is true that never before have I received such great consolation at the altar: the divine Child was visible there and yet invisible. Why should not the angels be there also? But I will tell you no more: there are too many people around us." Three days later, on December 28, at age 55, Bishop Francis de Sales rendered his soul back to God.

The beatification of St. Francis de Sales, which occurred the very year he died, was the first formal beatification ever held in St. Peter's Basilica. He was canonized in 1665, and was declared a Doctor of the Universal Church by Pope Pius IX in 1877. With this declaration the Church presented the teachings of St. Francis de Sales to all the faithful as a sure guide to true Catholic doctrine and the ways of the spiritual life—a sure guide to Heaven.

PREFACE

Although honored by the request to write an introduction to the sermons which are included in this volume, I have found the task to be a daunting one. St. Francis de Sales is the patron of our diocese and so deserving of our devotion and piety. He was the founder and is the continuing inspiration of a religious community which has served this and innumerable other dioceses in America, Europe and throughout the world with gentle charity and with loving concern for the poor and disadvantaged. He was a model bishop, making himself all things to all people. Long before the word came into popular usage, he actively engaged in the practice of the grassroots ecumenism which longs to see all Christians reunited in the bonds of charity and faith for which Jesus Himself prayed. He is the author of several volumes of sermons, treatises, conferences and informal conversations which have nourished the spiritual lives of Christians for over three hundred and fifty years. Over and above all these admirable accomplishments, he is a saint and a Doctor of the Catholic Church. The mere telling of his spiritual, pastoral and personal qualities and accomplishments is enough to render any praise which I might offer to him unnecessary and superfluous. Equally, it should convince my readers that the words of St. Francis de Sales which they will find in this volume are words of life, vibrant echoes of the words of Jesus and of the Spirit whom Jesus sent to the Church for its guidance and holiness.

The sermons presented in this small book are those delivered by St. Francis for the Sundays and feasts of the liturgical year beginning with the Second Sunday of Advent and concluding with the Second Sunday after the Epiphany. They were spoken, for the most part, during the period 1620-1622,

one of them only three days before the Saint's final pilgrimage
to his Lord in Heaven. They are, thus, words which reveal
to us the fullness of Francis' mature pastoral concern, his
personal love of the Incarnate Saviour and the engaging simplicity with which he addressed his audience. His procedure
is to comment on the Gospel selection read in the Mass of
the day and to use its message as a springboard for instruction on the practical aspects of Christian conduct in everyday
life. These sermons were delivered in the presence of a community of his beloved Sisters of the Visitation, to whom he
was both a father and spiritual director. They have the un-
complicated freshness and informality of one who feels
thoroughly at home with his audience, before whom he is
completely himself and for whose benefit he pours out his
whole heart and spirit.

With Francis, we shall not find that formal and ornate rhe-
torical style which characterizes so many 17th-century sermons. Rather, he is content to follow the advice which he
gave to St. Jeanne de Chantal's brother, Andre Fremyot, when
the latter was named Archbishop of Bourges: "To speak well,
it is enough to love well." Accustomed as he was to making
use of homely, down to earth and, sometimes, legendary examples to convey his message, he is, in these sermons, as
he himself said in another context, a "barber and not a sur-
geon," by which he meant to say: "When I am preaching
in the choir before seculars, I give no pain. I only throw
perfumes, I only speak of virtues and of matters likely to
console our hearts; I play a little on the flute and dwell on
the praises which we ought to render to God." (*Spiritual Conferences of St. Francis de Sales*, Gasquet-Mackey, Conf.
XVI—"On Antipathies," p. 238). His words are thus intended
for all Christians, regardless of their state or position in life.
Although aware of human faults and frailties, he habitually
emphasizes the love of God as the true pole star of Christian
life, and he gently, yet constantly, encourages his hearers to
focus their lives and their vision on its unfailing light.

Readers of these pages will, perhaps, be struck by the length of Francis' sermons, for they are habitually longer than those which are common in our day. They will want to note, at the same time, the richness and the wide range of his thought. Drawing on both the Old and the New Testaments, the writing of the Fathers of the Church, the lives of the Saints, and sometimes on examples found in classical literature, he weaves an extraordinarily full and colorful tapestry of thought, against which the simple words of the Gospel text come to life and receive brilliant illumination. While styles and taste in preaching change with the centuries (for they should be adapted to their own times and their own audiences), the message of the Gospel, which is Francis' chief concern, does not change. His words are as meaningful to Christians of our times as they were to those of the 17th century.

Above all else, however, readers of these pages should allow the gentle and devoted spirit of St. Francis de Sales to touch their hearts and minds as he touched the hearts and minds of his own audiences. That spirit is a spirit on which has been indelibly impressed a tender and deep devotion to the God who is Creator, Redeemer and Sanctifier of each and every member of the human race. It is a spirit suffused with that wisdom which looks beyond the surface of persons and events and sees the ever present Providence of God in human affairs. It is a spirit which burns bright with a consuming love for our Lord and Saviour, for Him who gave His life that we might find life in Him. It is a spirit shot through with love for the Church, for its unity, for its members united to Jesus Christ as the tendrils of the vine are united to its stock. It is a spirit which willingly recognizes the value of all that is truly human in each individual and consistently encourages its growth and development. It is a spirit which is humble, simple, clear-eyed in its perception of human limitations and yet convinced that God, in His infinite mercy, has called each and every one of His human creatures to enjoy friendship with Him in this life and throughout all eternity. It is the spirit of the pastoral bishop whom St. Francis, unconsciously depicting his own self-portrait, described as "a man gentle, charitable, and zealous for God's glory, a vigilant pastor; in short, a man perfect in every virtue and one who performs carefully all the duties of his office, having the two natures of his soul so well ordered that there is nothing of hatred in him except for sin and nothing of love except for the love of our dear Saviour." (Sermon for December 6, 1620, p. 17-18 of this volume).

I express my gratitude to the Sisters of the Visitation who have labored lovingly over the translation of these sermons. In making them available to the members of their own communities, they have also made them available to the entire English-speaking Church. This service is yet one more manifestation of their devotion to the Church and to its members, a devotion of which I and all the members of the Diocese of Wilmington are gratefully conscious. May God grant that each of us who reads these pages will be animated with St. Francis de Sales' "spirit of compassion to befriend all on the way to salvation." (Mass of St. Francis de Sales, January 24).

Robert E. Mulvee
Bishop of Wilmington

Feast of the Transfiguration
August 6, 1987

TRANSLATOR'S NOTE

The nine sermons for Advent and Christmas contained in this book were translated from St. Francis de Sales' *Oeuvres*, Tomes 8, 9 and 10 (Annecy: Niérat, 1892-1964).

The first volume of this series, *Sermons of St. Francis de Sales on Prayer*, includes an Introduction on the Origins and Value of the Sermons which was also taken from the Annecy edition.

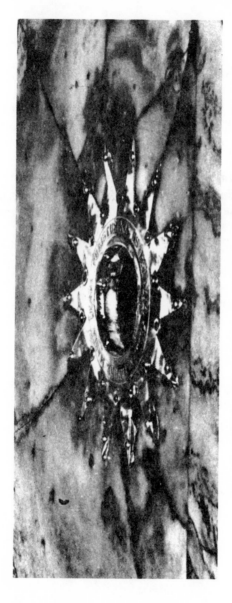

Silver star marking the spot of the birth of Our Lord in Bethlehem; it was here that the Virgin Mary first beheld the Infant Jesus as He lay on the ground. The star was placed on this spot in 1717, replacing an earlier marker. It is 56 centimeters in diameter and has 14 points in accord with the genealogy in *Matthew* 1:17. Mystically symbolic of Christ's divinity, it bears the Latin inscription, *Hic de Virgine Maria Jesus Christus natus est.*

SAINT JOHN THE BAPTIST SENDS HIS DISCIPLES TO JESUS

Sermon for the Second Sunday of Advent, December 6, 1620, concerning why St. John sent his disciples to ask Jesus if He were the Messias although he already knew He was, three reasons why God asks questions, John's desire to make Jesus known to the whole world, to guide his disciples directly to Jesus and to detach his disciples from himself, how St. John adapted himself to his disciples' weakness, how St. Paul adapted his instruction to his hearers, how Our Lord identified Himself by pointing to His works, the spiritual significance of these works: the blind see, the lame walk, lepers are cured, the deaf hear, dead men are resuscitated and the poor have the Gospel preached to them, the "scandal" of the Cross and its necessity for salvation, Our Lord's praise of St. John the Baptist and the reasons He did not deliver it in the presence of John's disciples, St. John's unshakable spiritual stability and our fickleness, and St. Ambrose's great meekness yet unshakable firmness.

"Are you he who is to come or are we to look for another?" —Matt. 11:3

Today's Gospel [*Matt.* 11:2-10] is divided into three parts, each of which we shall speak about now. The first treats of how St. John, while imprisoned for the truth, sent two of his disciples [*Lk.* 7:19] to Our Lord to learn whether He was the promised Messias or whether they were to look for another. The second concerns the Saviour's response to them.

1

And the third concerns what is said of St. John after the departure of his disciples.

It is truly amazing that our ancient Fathers, though so discerning and so insightful in explaining and developing even the most obscure difficulties presented by Holy Scripture, nevertheless find themselves wondering how to understand the first part of today's Gospel: that St. John, who knew Our Lord, nevertheless sent his disciples to learn if He were that great Prophet, that promised Messias, or if they should look for another. For, they ask, since St. John certainly knew that He was indeed the Messias, why does he send someone to ask Him that?

There is no doubt that he knew that the One to whom he sent his envoys was truly the Messias. For he knew Him while he was still in his mother's womb, and there is no saint with a more penetrating knowledge of the mystery of the Incarnation than this glorious St. John. He was Our Lady's pupil. He was sanctified by the dear Saviour of our souls when Our Lady went to visit her cousin Elizabeth. He surely knew Him from that moment and, leaping with joy in his mother's womb [*Lk.* 1:41, 42], he adored Him and consecrated himself to His service. He was His Precursor, and announced His coming to the world. It was he who baptized Him, who saw the Holy Spirit descend as a dove on Him and who heard the voice of the Father saying: "This is My beloved Son, in whom I am well pleased." It is he who pointed Him out in these words: "Behold the Lamb of God who takes away the sin of the world!" [*Matt.* 3:13-17; *Jn.* 1:29-36].

Thus he indeed knew Our Lord and never wavered in the least regarding who He was and in his belief and certitude of His coming. Then why, ask our ancient Fathers, does John, while in prison and hearing of the great prodigies and miracles wrought by our Divine Master, send his disciples to learn who He is and whether it is He who is to come or if they are to wait for another? Certainly, they all unravel the difficulty admirably. And if I wanted to relate to you their many and varied opinions on this topic it would take too much time and rob us of that which we wish to use for our instruction. I shall pause only long enough to give what two of our greatest Doctors, St. Hilary and St. Chrysostom, say about it. It seems to me that they have hit the nail right on the head and have gone straight to the point of the truth.

These holy Fathers say that we do not ask questions always to learn something, or because we are ignorant of what we ask. There are many other purposes and reasons for our questions. Otherwise the Divine Majesty would never have asked any question, since He knows everything and cannot be ignorant of anything whatsoever. He penetrates the inmost depths of the heart and there is nothing, however secret or hidden, that is not most clear and manifest to that Divine Wisdom. [*Ecclus.(Sir.)* 42:18-20; *Heb.* 4:13]. That is what the Royal Prophet David, that great and divine poet, says in his Psalm: O Lord, my path and my line You have searched out. [*Ps.* 138(139):1-9]. As if he said: "Though I am shrewd as a fox, nevertheless You penetrate all my shrewdness. Though I have been like a stag that has run and leaped through impenetrable thickets, surrounded by thorns and briars, You are the Divine Hunter who has nevertheless observed all my progress and my traces; You saw from afar where I was, for Your eyes see and penetrate everything. What shall I do to conceal myself from You? If I ascend into Heaven, You are there; and there I shall find You much more present than I am to myself. If, like the break of day and the beautiful dawn, I fly over the waters, You will be there sooner than I. I cannot escape from before Your face; what shall I do then, O Lord?"

From this it is clear that God knows all things, and yet He has asked many questions of people; His Divine Providence asked these questions for three different reasons. First, in order to make them confess their sins. He did this when Adam transgressed His commandment. He called him, saying to him: "Adam. Where are you?" and demanded of our first mother, Eve, what she had done. [*Gen.* 3:9, 13]. It was certainly not because He did not know where Adam was,

or the act of disobedience that he had committed. The Lord
questioned him in order to make him acknowledge his fault
so that He might pardon him. And instead of confessing it,
that miserable man threw the blame on his wife. [*Gen.* 3:12].
Because he did not confess his sin, he with all his posterity
was chastised by God. Some of the Fathers hold that if, when
God called him, he had confessed his sin, if he had struck
his breast and said a fervent *Peccavi,* "I have sinned"[1]
[2 *Kgs.*(2 *Sam.*) 12:13], the Lord would have pardoned him
and would not have chastised him with the scourge with which
He punished him with all his descendants. But inasmuch as
he did not do so, we remain stained with the sin of our first
parents and are consequently subject to the penalty that he
drew upon himself.

The second reason why the Divine Majesty poses questions to men is to enlighten them or instruct them on what
concerns the mysteries of Faith, as He did in the case of
the two disciples on the way to Emmaus. [*Lk.* 24:15, 17, 25-27].
Appearing to them in the guise of a pilgrim, He asked them
what they were talking about, questioning them and enlight-
ening them on the doubt they were experiencing concerning
His Resurrection. He did not, then, ask them about their
conversation because He was ignorant of what they were speaking, but rather so that by confessing their ignorance and their
doubts they might be instructed and enlightened.

The third reason why questions can be asked is to provoke
love. For example, Magdalen, after the Death and Passion
of Our Lord, went to anoint and embalm His sacred body.
[*Mk.* 16:1]. Finding the tomb opened, she wept bitterly. She
saw two angels there. They asked her, "Woman, why are
you weeping?" "Alas," she replied, "because they have taken
away my Lord and I do not know where they have laid Him."
Then, going a little further, she came upon Our Lord in the
guise of a gardener. He questioned her: "Woman, why are
you weeping? Whom are you seeking?" [*Jn.* 20:11-15].

Certainly it is no surprise that the angels were puzzled
to see Magdalen weep, still less that they asked her why,

for they do not know how to weep. (Although it is said mystically that angels weep, Holy Scripture uses the expression [*Is.* 33:7] only to symbolize their terror at some formidable thing. But they do not weep.) Knowing that human nature is subject to tears, our dear Saviour asks this woman why she is weeping. And why, Lord, do You ask her? Do You not know very well the cause of her sorrow and for what she is searching? Surely, He knew all this quite well. It was not to find out that He questioned her, since all things are most clear and manifest to Him. [*Heb.* 4:13]. But this dear Saviour of our souls posed such and similar questions to elicit ejaculatory prayers and acts of love and union.

Therefore, we do not always ask questions only because of ignorance, to know or to find out something, but for different reasons. So the glorious St. John did not send his disciples to Our Lord to find out whether or not He was the Messias, for he had no doubt about that. He had three reasons for sending those disciples to Jesus.

First, to make Him known to the whole world. He had already spent time preaching His coming, His miracles, and His greatness to his disciples. Now he wanted them to see Him whom he had announced to them. Surely, to make God known should be the principal aim of all doctors and preachers. Teachers and those who govern and have charge of souls ought neither to seek nor to obtain anything but this: that He whom they preach and in whose name they teach may be known to everyone. That was this glorious saint's wish.

The only sign by which God may be found and known is God Himself. At our Saviour's birth the angels sought out the shepherds and announced to them His coming, singing in a wonderfully pleasing melody these sacred and oft-repeated words: *Gloria in excelsis Deo.* But to confirm the miracle they had made known to them, they said: Go see Him, and then you will believe and hold for certain what we announce to you. [*Lk.* 2:10-14]. For there is no means nor certain sign for finding God but God Himself.[2] This is why our glorious saint, after having long preached to his disciples the coming

of Our Lord, now sends them to Him not only that they
may know Him, but still more that they may make Him known
to others.

The second reason he sent them was this: he did not want
to draw disciples to himself, but only to his Teacher, to whose
school he now sends them so that they might be instructed
personally by Him. For what else was he suggesting in this
sending but this: "Although I teach and preach to you, it
is not to attract you to myself, but rather to Jesus Christ,
whose voice I am. [*Jn.* 1:23]. That is why I am sending
you to Him. Learn from Him whether He is the promised
Messias, or whether you are to look for another." By this
John meant: "I am not content to assure you that it is He
whom we await. I am sending you that you may be instructed
by Him personally to that effect." Surely, doctors and
preachers, teachers of novices, and those who have charge
of souls have done something worthwhile only to the extent
that they have sent their disciples and those in their care
to Our Lord's school, to be plunged into His sea of knowledge. They were successful only to the degree that they urged
and persuaded others to seek out our dear Saviour to be instructed by Him personally. This is what the great Apostle
meant in writing to the Corinthians: My little children, whom
I have conceived and won for Jesus Christ amidst so many
pains, fatigues and labors, and for whom I have suffered so
much anguish and torment, I assure you that I did not teach
you so as to attract you to myself, but only so as to draw
you to my Lord Jesus Christ. [*1 Cor.* 4:9-16; cf. *Gal.* 4:19].

If teachers and those who have spiritual care of others try,
by beautiful words, to draw to themselves the disciples whom
they teach and the souls for whom they care, they are like
pagans, heretics, and others who talk and ramble on, and
who take great pains in the pulpit to deliver beautiful, subtle
and finely crafted discourses, whose sole purpose is not to
lead souls to Jesus Christ, but only to themselves! They attract others to themselves by their words and impressive language. There is no real substance here, only babbling and

cackling, yet they captivate many weak spirits in this way. True servants of God, on the contrary, preach and teach those whom they guide only so as to lead them to God, as much by their words as by their works. This is what St. John does today, and to this all superiors ought to pay careful attention. For they will never achieve success but by directing and sending their disciples to Our Lord to learn from Him what He is and to study under Him so as to know and to do what is necessary for His love and service.

The third reason St. John sent his disciples to Our Lord was to detach them from himself. He feared they would be led into the great error of esteeming him more than the Saviour. They were already complaining to St. John in this manner: Teacher, you and we, your disciples, along with the Pharisees, fast. We are poorly clothed and do great penance. But this man, this great prophet who performs so many miracles among us, does not do so. [*Matt.* 9:14; *Mk.* 2:18]. In hearing this, and in seeing that the love and esteem which his disciples felt for him was beginning to produce in them a feeling of contempt for Jesus Christ, St. John sent them to this Divine Majesty to be instructed and informed of the truth.

It was not, therefore, because St. John doubted in the least that Our Lord was the Messias that he sent his disciples to question Him. He sent them for their own benefit and advantage and to make Him known to the whole world; not to draw them to himself but to detach them from him; to let them see the miracles that Jesus Christ performed so that they might come to Him in a manner worthy of Him. He deals with them as befits their status as still children. He assuredly believed that Jesus is the Son of God, the Lamb of God who takes away the sin of the world.[3] [*Jn.* 1:29]. And certainly he could, by his own words, have brought them to understand this truth, but he chose to direct them to Our Lord for this instruction. He could have sent them to Him to adore and confess Him; but, accommodating himself to their weakness and infirmity, he sent them only to ask Him

who He is and whether He is "He who is to come" or whether
they should look for another. Surely those who direct souls
must make themselves all things to all men, as the Apostle
says to save all [*1 Cor.* 9:19-22]. Let them be gentle with
some and severe with others, children with children, strong
with the strong, weak with the weak; in short, they need
great discretion so as to accommodate themselves to each
one's need.

St. Paul himself practiced this marvelously, for he made
himself as a child with children, and for this reason he often
addressed Christians as "my little children." [*Gal.* 4:19]. Writing to the Thessalonians he said: My little children, I became as a little one in the midst of you, so that I might
save all of you. I walked with little steps, and not with the
steps of a great Apostle. For you would hardly have been
able to follow such steps, being little children. I adapted myself to your weakness, and I walked slowly with you as a
little child. Furthermore, I have been in your midst as a nursing
mother [*1 Thess.* 2:7-8]; I gave you milk to drink and nourished
you with food suited to your littleness. [*1 Cor.* 3:1-2].

St. John Chrysostom, Bishop of Constantinople, outstanding in all he wrote, but particularly on the subject of this
Apostle, said in the beginning of a sermon on the Epistle
to the Hebrews (I do not know if I can recall it exactly):
"Here is an amazing thing; when this great Apostle was among
his Corinthians, he was like a nursing mother among her
children. He nourished them with simple food, which was
sweet and suited to little children. On the contrary, when
he wrote to the Hebrews it was with a doctrine so profound,
and a style so elevated, that it is without parallel."

If you want to understand how St. Paul was in the midst
of the Corinthians,[4] look at a mother who has five or six
children around her. Notice this woman's skill, how she can
give to each one what is appropriate and can treat each one
according to his understanding. To the one who is only one,
two or three years old she gives milk; she uses baby talk
with him and plays with him. She does not expect him to say

"father" and "mother" but only "papa" and "mama." Being so very young, he cannot yet pronounce the words "father" and "mother." Those that are four or five years old she teaches to talk better and to eat more solid food. Those a little older she instructs in courtesy and modesty.

"Now," writes this holy Father, "when the great Apostle said, 'I am among you as a nursing mother,' what does he mean but that he acts toward his disciples as a nursing mother does toward her children?" It is certainly necessary for those who guide souls to have great zeal to learn all that is required to guide them according to their capacity and attraction. They must use great discernment so as to give them the food of God's word at the fitting and appropriate time so that it may be well received, and again great discernment to give each one what he needs and in the way best suited to him. Let no one say, "You do not speak to me for my perfection as much as you do to this other person." I reply, "I do not think you have enough teeth to handle the practices that are recommended to others.[5] You could not masticate them." You answer, "I think I do have enough teeth." "Surely, you have even fewer than you think since you believe you have more! Ah, then, let yourself be governed by others." And this is my first point.

The second part of our Gospel is the response Our Lord made to John's disciples. Reflecting on this response, some Doctors have been astonished. Relate to John what you have heard and seen; the blind see, the lame walk, lepers are cured, the deaf hear, dead men are resuscitated and the poor have the Gospel preached to them. (That the poor have the Gospel preached to them is considered a miracle here.) These Doctors note that the Saviour did not work many miracles in the presence of John's disciples, but that the Apostles told them of those He had worked. Most certainly, the Apostles delighted in relating the wonderful works of their good Master to these two disciples. But Our Lord also performed many miracles in their presence, which is why He answered them: Relate to John what you hear and see.

Some of our early Fathers, namely St. Hilary and St. Chrysostom, dwell upon this answer which Our Lord gave to those who asked Him who He was. "You ask Me whether I am that great Prophet, the promised Messias, He who thunders in the heavens [cf. *2 Kgs.* (*2 Sam.*) 22:14] and who is to come to crush the head of the enemy. [*Gen.* 3:15]. I answer you: Relate what you have heard and seen." Oh wonderful humility of our dear Saviour who comes to confound our pride and to destroy our false sense of superiority! They ask Him: "Who are You?" and His only answer is: "Relate what you have heard and seen." He answers thus to teach us that it is our works and not our words that give testimony to what we are, we who are so full of pride.

If anyone were to ask a gentleman today, "Who are you?" he would consider such a question a challenge to his honor and would no doubt cut his questioner's throat on the spot! "Who are you?" "Must I show you my lineage and ancestry? Must I produce my pedigree for you? Must I demonstrate whether my ancestors are descended from Abraham, Isaac and Jacob?" (Such silliness is absolute nonsense!) Surely, there is no need whatsoever of displaying all these nothings to prove that you are a gentleman. But when asked the question: "Who are you?" you must reply: "Relate what you see, a man gentle, cordial, benevolent, the protector of widows, the father of orphans and minors, charitable and benign towards his subjects. If you have seen and heard such things, say assuredly that you have seen a real gentleman." If you address yourself to a bishop: "Who are you?" he should be able to render this testimony of himself: "Relate that you see a man who fulfills his charge well and devoutly." Then you may be assured that he is truly a bishop. If a religious is asked: "Who are you?" and if she is seen to be exact and punctual in the observance of her rules, she can answer that she is truly a religious. In short, it is our works, whether good or bad, that form us, and it is by them that we ought to be recognized.

When asked, "Who are you?" do not be content to answer

like little children in catechism class: "I am a Christian";
rather, live in such a manner that one will recognize clearly
in you a person who loves God with his whole heart, one
who keeps the Commandments, frequents the Sacraments,
and does all things worthy of a true Christian. I do not mean
that when we are asked who we are we must not say that
we are Christians. Oh, certainly not! It is the most beautiful
title we can give ourselves. I have always had a special devotion to that great St. Blandina who was martyred at Lyon
and whose life was written by Eusebius. Amidst all the ex-
cruciating torments of her martyrdom, she kept repeating
gently, "I am a Christian," making use of this word as a
sacred balm to heal all her wounds. All I mean is that it
is not enough to be *called* a Christian if we do not perform
the works of a Christian. After all, what are we? A little
dust and ashes. [*Gen.* 3:19; 18:27].

Let us, then, candidly admit that we are nothing, that we
can do nothing, that we know nothing. What nonsense that,
being what we are, we nevertheless wish to make a show
and to walk on tiptoe in order to be seen by everyone! But
what will they actually see in seeing us? A little dust and
a body all too soon corrupted in death!

"Tell John that the blind see." O God, what greater blindness than ours. Though full of abjection and misery, we
nevertheless wish to be esteemed something! What can blind
us in this way except self-love which, besides being blind
itself, also blinds the one in whom it dwells? Those who
paint Cupid always cover his eyes to indicate that love is
blind. This should be understood still more of self-love, which
is blind to its own abjection and the nothingness, from which
it proceeds and of which it is formed. Surely, it is a great
grace and sign of interior conversion when God gives us His
light to know our misery. He who truly knows himself is
not annoyed when he is held and treated for what he is. For
he has received that light which frees him of his blindness.

"Tell John that the lame walk." Whether the infirm of whom
Our Lord speaks here were lame in one limb or both scarcely

matters. But most of those who live in this world are lame in both. We all have two natures which are like our two legs. These two natures are the irascible and the concupiscible. When they are not well-regulated and mortified, they render a person lame. The concupiscible nature covets wealth, honors, dignities, preeminence, pleasures and delicacies, and renders a person covetous and avaricious, causing him to limp to one side.

There are others who, though not avaricious, have so strong an irascible nature that when it is not rightly submissive to reason, it causes them to be troubled, and to resent inordinately the least things done to them. They get up their guard and continually look for ways to avenge themselves for any little word or wrong done them. Now, to whatever side it turns, be it good or bad, this nature is very strong; but when it turns to the side of evil, it is difficult indeed to set it right. Very many have both natures damaged, and these limp on both sides; others limp on only one. Our Lord came to cure the lame; He came to make them walk upright before His face in the observance of His Commandments. [Cf. *Lk.* 1:6]. Therefore He adds: Relate to John that the lame walk.

"Tell John that lepers are cured." There are a great many spiritual lepers in the world. This evil is a certain languor and tepidity in God's service. Persons thus afflicted have neither a fever nor a life-threatening illness, but their bodies are so infected with this leprosy that they are completely enfeebled and broken down. By this I mean that they have no major imperfections and commit no grave faults, but they do commit and omit so many little ones that their heart remains quite weak and languid. And the most dangerous thing of all is that while in this state they cannot be touched or moved without being pricked to the heart. Surely, those infected with this leprosy are very much like little lizards, vile and abject animals, the feeblest and simplest of all. Yet despite their weakness and infirmity, they immediately turn to bite us if we touch them ever so lightly. Spiritual lepers act the same. Although they are covered over with an infinite number of minutely small imperfections, they are so haughty that they do not want to be seen nor touched in any way. And if you rebuke them ever so slightly, they immediately turn to bite you.

"Tell John that the deaf hear." There is a spiritual deafness that is very dangerous. It is a certain vain complacency in ourselves and in what we do, so that, it seems to us, we no longer need any growth or improvement. We are no longer anxious to hear the word of God preached, or to read books of devotion, or to be reproved or corrected; we amuse ourselves with trifles, thereby placing ourselves in great peril. If it is a very good sign when a person listens willingly to the divine word, is it not a bad sign when she is disgusted with it and no longer feels she needs it?

"Tell John that dead men are resuscitated." Actually, it is this sacred word that resuscitates the dead. It is by listening to preaching that we receive good inspirations and pass from sin to grace. It is by good reading, too, that the heart comes alive and ever gains new strength and vigor.

"Tell John that the poor have the Gospel preached to them." Some say: The poor preach the Gospel. Whichever way we interpret it, it is almost one and the same thing; yet I prefer to keep to the text of our Gospel and say with Our Lord: the poor have the Gospel preached to them. Surely, St. John's disciples did not find Our Lord among the princes and leaders of the world, but with the poor, who listened to Him and followed Him wherever He went. This dear Saviour of our souls came for the poor and took a singular pleasure in being with them. O God, with what gentleness He taught them! He made Himself all things to all men in order to save all.[6] [*1 Cor.* 9:22]. He gives His Spirit to the poor and humble [*Is.* 61:1; *Lk.* 4:18] because poverty engenders humility. He flees the proud and haughty of heart, and gives Himself to the simple. [Cf. *Wis.* 1:5]. He lifts their heavy and sluggish spirit and gives them His own, with which they can do great things. [Cf. *Ps.* 103(104):29-30]. Thus

He confounds the high and mighty by the lowly and simple.
[*1 Cor.* 1:27-28]. For this reason we can say in truth not only
that the poor have the Gospel preached to them, but also
that they preach the Gospel, God using them to carry His
truth to the whole world.

It is indeed true that our dear Saviour and Master came
to teach both the little and the great, the learned and the
simple. Yet we almost always find Him among the poor and
simple. How different is God's Spirit from that of the world,
which esteems only appearance and pomp. Ancient
philosophers received into their schools only those who had
a good mind and sound judgment. Of those who did not
possess these qualities they said openly, "Such a canvas is
not suited to our brush." Today we see many simple folk
despised by some people who become irritated and wearied
by their conversation and who take pleasure only in being
among lofty minds. No matter how haughty, proud and arrogant these people may be, the world still tolerates them. But
God's Spirit does quite the contrary; It rejects the proud and
converses with the humble. Our Lord even numbers this among
His miracles: "Relate to John that the poor have the Gospel
preached to them."

Then He adds: "Blessed is he who will not be scandalized
in Me." What do You mean here, O Lord? How could it
be possible for anyone to be scandalized after having seen
You perform so many miracles and works of such great charity and mercy?[7] "I will be," says the Lord, "the disgrace
of men, the outcast of the people [*Ps.* 21(22):7]; I will be
a scandal to the Jews and a stone of stumbling to Gentiles.
[*1 Cor.* 1:23; *Rom.* 9:33; *1 Ptr.* 2:7-8]. But blessed is he
who will not be scandalized in Me. For I, who am now work-
ing such great miracles in your midst, must be crucified and
attached to a Cross. Because of that many will be scandalized." Oh, blessed are those who will not be scandalized
at Our Lord's humiliations and ignominies when they see
Him outcast and everybody's laughingstock. Blessed are they
who, during this life, crucify themselves with Him, meditating

on His Passion and bearing in themselves His mortification. [*2 Cor.* 4:10].

Indeed, we must all go this route. We must attach ourselves to our Saviour's Cross, meditate on it, and bear in ourselves His mortification. There is no other road to Heaven. Our Lord travelled it first. Experience as many ecstasies, spiritual raptures and transports as you wish; even ravish the Eternal Father's Heart if you are able. Yet if with all this you do not dwell on the Saviour's Cross and practice self-mortification, I assure you that all the rest is absolutely nothing and will disappear in smoke and vanity; and you, in turn, will remain empty of all good, permitting yourselves to be scandalized at Our Lord's Passion as were many of His contemporaries. In short, there is no other gate to Heaven than that of humiliation and mortification.

Let me bring all this to a conclusion. The disciples, then, returned to St. John to relate what they had seen and heard. O God,[8] think of the hearts of these good disciples! How peaceful and filled with great consolation! How they must have tarried with their master, telling him everything they had seen and heard! How filled they must have been with great insights and knowledge concerning Our Lord's coming! How tenderly they must have conversed with one another about those wonderful miracles and prodigies He performed in their presence and those things related to them by the Apostles!

As they were setting out, the Saviour turned to those around Him and asked: What did you go out to the desert to see? Perhaps you went there to see a reed exposed to storms and tempests, or truly a rock immovable in the midst of the sea? (Similarly, we might ask: What did you go to see in the desert, that is, in religious life? For the desert is related to the origins of religious life, and religious life is nothing else but a desert of sorts.) So, what did you go out to see? Perhaps you found reeds there? Oh, no, St. John is not a reed, for he dwelt there like a rock, immovable in the midst of all the waves and tempests of tribulation.

But why did Our Lord not praise His Precursor in the presence of his disciples? Our ancient Fathers say that there were two reasons for this. First, because these good disciples were too attached to their master; they were captivated by him, and their esteem was so great as to prefer him to Jesus Christ, as when they said to John:[9] You and we, your disciples, perform great penances; but this Prophet, who is in our midst, does not. [*Matt.* 9:14; *Mk.* 2:18]. Obviously, they loved St. John greatly and had no need of Our Lord's praising him in their presence, for there was danger of their valuing him more highly than the Saviour. This is why this Divine Wisdom said nothing about him in their presence.

The other reason was because our Divine Master was no flatterer. If He had praised St. John, they might have thought He did it through flattery so that it might be brought back to him by his two disciples. This was very foreign to our dear Saviour's spirit. He is Truth Itself. The human spirit of John's disciples might also have added a little something on the subject. That is why He who sees all knew what could happen and did not praise him in the presence of his disciples.

But when they had departed, He asked the Jews: What did you go out to the desert to see? Consider this man whom you have seen, or rather this angel clothed in human form. You have found in him not a reed, but a firm rock, a man possessed of unshakable stability in the midst of all sorts of changing circumstances. This is the most agreeable and desirable virtue in the spiritual life.[10] You did not see a reed, for St. John is the same in adversity as in prosperity, the same in prison amidst persecutions as in the desert amidst applause; as joyous in the winter of trouble as in the springtime of peace; he fulfilled the same role in prison as he did in the desert!

We, on the contrary, are forever changing. We vary according to time and season. There are some people so changeable that when the weather is fine, nothing can equal their joy; but when stormy, nothing can equal their depression. Such

people who are fervent, prompt and optimistic in prosperity
will be weak, depressed and disheartened in adversity. It would
then take Heaven and earth to restore them to peace, and
ordinarily even then all our efforts are useless. You will find
others who want only happy times because at such times they
do marvels, or so it seems to them. Others prefer adversity.
Tribulation, they say, keeps them close to God. In short, we
are spiritually fickle and really do not know what we want.
There are some who, when in consolation, cannot be re-
strained, but when sad, cannot be consoled. When we contradict them in nothing, O God, they are so strong and do
such marvels! But if we touch them, if we contradict them
in the slightest thing, all is lost. It is so difficult for us to
be receptive even to the littlest thing which is contrary to
our liking that our peace of soul cannot be restored until
long afterwards, and many salves must be used. My God,
what a shame that we are so inconstant! Surely, there is no
stability in us, and yet this is the most essential quality in
the spiritual life. We are reeds, tossed about in every direction by every mood and humor.

I shall finish by applying to the glorious St. Ambrose, the
first Vespers of whose feast we are celebrating today, what
Our Lord said in reference to St. John the Baptist: You have
not seen a reed in the desert. You should have a special devotion to St. Ambrose because he was St. Augustine's spiritual
father. In his *Confessions,* St. Augustine tells us that not only
St. Ambrose's learned preaching, but especially his meekness and gentleness, stole his heart away. He was French;
that is, he was born in France, although St. Augustine met
him in Milan. It is related in one of his biographies that
while he was yet an infant, a swarm of bees formed a honeycomb on his lips—thus predicting a gentle and meek future
for him. If we were to ask this glorious saint, "Who are
you?" [*Jn.* 1:19] without doubt he would reply, "Relate what
you have seen and heard. Relate that you have seen a man
gentle, charitable and zealous for God's glory, a vigilant pastor;
in short, a man perfect in every virtue and one who performs

carefully all the duties of his office, having the two natures of his soul so well ordered that there is nothing of hatred in him except for sin, and nothing of love except for the love of our dear Saviour."

Although he was extremely gentle and merciful, he was also very severe in punishing and reproving what was deserving of reprehension, never permitting himself to flinch before any consideration whatever. What zeal did he not display in his treatment of the Emperor Theodosius, refusing him entrance into the Church and speaking to him with great severity, never wavering until the Emperor had confessed his fault. And when he was reminded that it was an emperor he was reprehending, he testified that he regarded only God's glory.

At the time of this incident, some reminded Ambrose of King David's fault. "Ah, indeed," he answered, "you speak to me of David's fault, but you make no mention of his penitence. If the Emperor wishes to do as he did, the doors of the Church will be opened to him; otherwise, no."[11] And he showed indeed that without regard for king or emperor, he would remain firm in the exercise of his office. Relate then what you have seen and heard; for the fame of this great saint spread everywhere, so that very learned and experienced men came from great distances to hear his doctrine.

How true it is that man is known by his works![12] So if we want to know what we are, we must look into our actions, reforming what is not good and perfecting what is, so that in imitating these two glorious saints in their virtues, we may enjoy with them the glory of Heaven.

In the name of the Father, and of the Son, and of the Holy Spirit. Amen.

NOTES

1. Cf. St. Francis de Sales: *Controversies,* published under the title *The Catholic Controversy,* translated by Rev. Henry Benedict Mackey, O.S.B., under the direction of Rt. Rev. John Cuthbert Hedley, O.S.B., Vol. III of Library of St. Francis de Sales (London: Burns and

Oates/New York: Catholic Publication Society Co., 1886), p. 7.

2. In a warm and simple manner, St. Francis de Sales is speaking here of the absolute priority of grace in the life of faith. Faith in God is the result neither of human nor angelic effort, but of God's grace—though God may use human and angelic agency to mediate that grace as He did with St. John the Baptist and the angels at Bethlehem.

3. Cf. p. 2 of this sermon.

4. Cf. St. Francis de Sales: *The Spiritual Conferences* (Westminster, Md: The Newman Press, 1962), XIII, "On the Spirit of the Rules," p. 254.

5. Obviously "not having enough teeth" is here equivalent to "not having the wherewithal" for a particular job or task. Here, as in so many cases, St. Francis is speaking with tongue in cheek, gleam in the eye and smile on his face. He is making it as easy as possible for some in his congregation to accept their spiritual shortcomings; he does it so gently!

6. Cf. p. 8 of this sermon.

7. Cf. *Controversies*, p. 6-7, 9.

8. The expressions "O God" and "O my God" are very characteristic of St. Francis de Sales, who lived and spoke in the presence of God.

9. Cf. p. 7 of this sermon.

10. Cf. *Spiritual Conferences*, III, "On Constancy."

11. St. Francis de Sales is alluding here to St. Ambrose's threat of excommunication to the Emperor Theodosius for the vengeful massacre of 7,000 defenseless people in the Circus of Thessalonica in punishment for a riot in which several imperial officers were killed. St. Ambrose insisted that the Emperor do public penance for his crime. He did. (Cf. *New Catholic Encyclopedia*, Vol. I, p. 374.)

12. Cf. p. 10 of this sermon.

2

THE GREAT HUMILITY
OF SAINT JOHN THE BAPTIST

Sermon for the Third Sunday of Advent, December 13, 1620, concerning pride and ambition as the most powerful temptations, the excellent humility of St. John the Baptist in renouncing the most dangerous and subtle temptation to pride and ambition, his immediate and succinct denial that he was the Messias, the desire of angels and of all men (even pagans) for the Incarnation, our foolish and untruthful acceptance of honors, St. John's humility in skillfully denying even the honored status that rightly belonged to him—without, however, being untruthful; how we should not excuse ourselves of the very faults we accuse ourselves of but confess them straightforwardly, humility's excellence, affinity with charity, and necessity in order to escape the devil's snares, St. John's lowly description of himself and Our Lord's praise of him, God's perennial humbling of the proud and favoring of the humble, and how all should imitate St. John the Baptist.

> *"Who are you? And he confessed, and did not deny: and he confessed: I am not the Christ." —Jn. 1:19-20*

If we are to judge by every art, business and profession, we will have to confess that the principal and most powerful temptations are those to ambition, pride and arrogance. Lucifer used them to tempt our first parents. It is said that ambition is the worst of them all since it caused him to stumble from heaven[1] into Hell. Knowing from his own experience what powerful allurements pride and ambition are, he used them to tempt our first parents by offering them the forbidden fruit with such arrogance that they were sure that by eating it they would be like God. [*Gen.* 3:5]. He did not tell them that they would be God's equal, for "Who is like God?" [Ps. 34 (35):10; 112 (113):5; *Is.* 40:18]. It is impossible to be God's equal; and if the miserable wretch had tempted Adam and Eve in that way, they would easily have recognized his deception, for being still in Original Justice, they were greatly gifted with perception and knowledge. This is why he said to them: "You will be like God." And how would they be like God? In eating this fruit they would, like God, know good and evil. Now this ambition so puffed up their pride that they actually presumed to share in divine wisdom and knowledge and allowed themselves to be seduced by the tempter. In this way they forfeited Original Justice.

Reflecting on the cause of the fall of Lucifer and the other angels,[2] some theologians say it was due to a certain spiritual self-complacency which, through an awareness of their angelic nature's grandeur and excellence, caused such self-pride that they desired with insupportable arrogance to be like God and to place their thrones on an equality with His. [Cf. *Is.* 14:13-14]. Others maintain that envy was the cause of their fall. They knew that the Lord would create human beings, that He willed to enrich human nature, and that, further, He would actually communicate Himself to this nature, incarnating and uniting Himself to it in hypostatic union in such manner that these two natures would form only one person. Knowing this, they were moved with envy. They were upset that the Creator planned to elevate human nature above theirs and said among themselves: "If God desires to go out of Himself so as to communicate Himself to another, why does He not choose an angelic and seraphic nature for this communication? Is it not far nobler and more excellent than the other?" From that moment on they were filled with jealousy, ambition and pride, and finally stumbled miserably.

But to what purpose do I say all this except to contrast it with and exalt the humility of St. John the Baptist, who is one of the persons who took part in the mystery of the Visitation and whose humility, it seems to me, is the most excellent and the most perfect that has ever been, after that of Our Lord and the most sacred Virgin? There was presented to him the strongest and most violent temptation imaginable to pride and ambition. But notice, I beg you, that it was not presented to him in person by the enemy and that it did not come from him directly. When an enemy is discovered or we see that a temptation comes from an adversary, we immediately become suspicious of whatever he says or whatever he urges us to do. Why? Because it is suggested to us by our enemy and therefore is not to be trusted.

It is most certain that if Adam and Eve had recognized their tempter, they would not have allowed themselves to be seduced. But this wicked spirit always uses trickery, knowing that if he does not disguise himself and assume some mask or the form of a friend when he makes an attack, he will never succeed. He seduces many by his wiles and cunning. When he presented himself to Eve, it was in the form of a serpent. [*Gen.* 3:1]. But at that time, serpents were not serpents as we now know them. They did not bite and had no venom. Consequently, Eve had no more fear of him than a small child would have of a young eagle. The enemy spoke to her in the form of a serpent and kindled in her the ambition and eager desire to be like God. For this reason she ate the forbidden fruit.

As for Lucifer and his angels, they had no other tempter than themselves, for as yet there was no devil. They were tempted by themselves. Because of pride they, who were once angels, became demons. For this reason we can rightly say that ambition, pride and arrogance came down from heaven[3] to the earthly paradise and from this paradise spread into the whole world, rendering it thereby an earthly hell. Thus the angel became a devil; he who had been beautiful and God's friend declared himself God's enemy and became ugly and horrible. Man, by pride and arrogance, lost the Original Justice in which he was created and made this earth a hell. For the evils that human vice draws in its wake are a veritable hell which lead from temporal to eternal punishment.

Notice how one of the strongest, most subtle and most dangerous temptations possible is being addressed to St. John, not by his enemies, as I have said before, nor by men assuming the mask of hypocrisy, but by his friends, sent to him from Jerusalem by the princes and doctors of the Law. Jerusalem was the royal city where the holy senate and judges resided. Scribes were the doctors of the Law, and Pharisees were like our priests and religious. The princes among the priests and the doctors governed the whole republic by the Law of Moses. These, then, sent people to St. John. But whom did they send? Perhaps some of their sons' valets or some other such men of low rank? Certainly not! They sent doctors and religious men as their ambassadors and those of the republic. And why? Simply to find out if John was actually the Christ, the Son of God, the Messias whom they were awaiting, so as to pay him due honor.

Notice, I pray you, the caprice of the human spirit. They were awaiting the Messias and they saw that all the prophecies had been fulfilled, for they had the Sacred Scripture at their fingertips. The Saviour came, and went among them teaching His doctrine, performing miracles and confirming by deed all that He said. Nevertheless, instead of acknowledging Him, they go in search of another!

They address themselves to the glorious St. John, asking him: Who are you? He told them and did not deny it: I am not the Christ. Are you Elias? No. Are you the Prophet? No. He confessed and did not deny it. These are the words of the Evangelist [*Jn.* 1:19-21], brief and to the point as they are in everything they relate. Our ancient Fathers correctly remark that when these envoys asked: "Who are you?" they did not want to know simply who he was, but whether he was the expected Messias. Otherwise would St. John have replied that he was not the Christ, if he had not believed that they were sent precisely in order to confess him as such? It is true that he was not, "and he confessed and did not deny it."

But reflect a little upon the truly perfect humility of this glorious saint. He rejected not only the honors, the preeminence and titles which did not apply to him but, what is more amazing, even those that he could have accepted. He, being like the rest of us, was certainly capable of committing venial sins.[4] And yet he had attained such a degree of humility that he triumphed beautifully over every pride and ambition, spurning and refusing to accept all the dignities and honors offered to him.

While in heaven, the angels never sought to be gods. Lucifer was too good a philosopher ever to believe that that was possible. He understood completely that he could never be such, that it was simply impossible. No, his ambition never went that far. He knew that God would always be the first and would always be above him. In short, He was God, and Lucifer did not presume to be His equal. Nevertheless his pride led him so far as to want to be *like* God. [*Is.* 14:14]. Through such arrogance the miserable wretch, instead of becoming what he rashly presumed to be, fell from what he was and was driven out, banished forever from Heaven. He became a devil. In him devils began to be; before his fall there were none.

Being in Original Justice, our first parents in paradise never sinned, neither mortally like the fallen angels (for the first sin that they committed was mortal and consequently deserved eternal death), nor venially. Nevertheless, they listened to the ancient serpent [*Apoc.(Rev.)* 12:9] when he said that if they ate of the forbidden fruit they would be like God. This sole promise made by Satan so touched their hearts that they forgot the Lord's command and prohibition. Oh! what strong and dangerous attractions are both pride and ambition, capable of seducing the human heart to transgress God's law! As the great St. Ambrose says, truly one must be clothed and armed on all sides with humility if one wishes to enter into the combat and war against vice.

Our glorious St. John was indeed armed with this virtue.
O God, how wonderfully present it was in this great saint!
For he was neither in Heaven, nor in the earthly paradise,
but on fallen earth; he was not an angel, but only a man;
he was not in Original Justice and could have sinned venially.[5] And they did not propose to him simply to be *like* God,
they came to make him confess that he was the Christ, and
they were prepared to acknowledge him as such! But he re-
fused emphatically such acknowledgment. "He confessed and
he did not deny" says the Evangelist, that he was not the
Christ.

How great were both this temptation and the humility with
which he repulsed it. But please take note how the messengers
from the princely priests speak to him: "We are here, sent
in the name of the scribes and Pharisees and the whole republic, to say to you that the prophecies are fulfilled and that
the time has arrived for the Messias' coming. It is true that
we see among us many persons who live well and are very
virtuous, but we must confess that we have not beheld anyone like you or anyone whose works so delight our hearts.
In short, we believe that you are the promised Messias. If
you are He, we beg you neither to deny nor to hide it any
longer, for we have come to pay you the honor that you deserve." See, they place the agreement in his hands. If he
had wished to accept it, they would have acknowledged him
as the Christ. But surely this glorious saint was too great
a lover of truth to allow himself to be carried away by such
an ambition. If he had said he was the Messias, he would
have been a great liar, disloyal and unfaithful, for he would
be accepting an honor that was not due him.

These scribes and Pharisees declared that they were awaiting the promised Messias, the Desired of the Nations [*Ag.*
2:8, Douay] and Him whom Jacob called "the Desire of the
eternal hills." [*Gen.* 49:26]. Some ancient Fathers explain
these words by saying that they describe the desire of the
angels for the Incarnation; others hold that we should

understand by them the desire that God had from all eternity
to unite our human nature with the divine, a desire that He
communicated to both angels and men, though in different
ways. Some, such as the Patriarchs and Prophets, longed ar-
dently for Him, and by those longings raised to Heaven they
petitioned for the Incarnation of the Son of God. Solomon
in the Canticle of Canticles [*Cant.* 1:1(1:2)] expresses this
longing in the words of the spouse: "Let Him kiss me with
a kiss of His mouth." What does this kiss signify but the
hypostatic union of the human nature with the divine?[6] Others
desire it, too, but almost imperceptibly. For from time immemorial we find people seeking the Divinity. Not being able
to make an incarnate God, because that belongs to God alone,
they sought ways to fabricate deities. For this purpose they
erected images and idols which they adorned and regarded
as gods among them. Certainly I know that these were illu-
sions. But yet we see in them the desire that God had im-
planted in all hearts for the Incarnation of His Son, the desire
for the union of the divine nature with the human nature.
These priests and Levites, then, had reason for saying that
all prophecies had been fulfilled and that the time had come
when they should see Him who was the Desired of the nations.

Now they ask St. John: "Who are you? Are you not the
Christ whom we await?" And he confessed and did not deny
that he was not. Oh, how far was St. John's spirit from that
of our times! He did not discourse beautifully in replying
to these messengers; he contented himself by simply answer-
ing that he was not the Christ. Surely, if they had wanted
to know simply what his profession was, without doubt they
would have been informed of the truth, and with more words.
But since they took him for what he was not, he succinctly
stated that he was not the one whom they thought him to be.

We, on the other hand, are extremely receptive to the honors
that are extended us! Our human nature is anxious to attract
whatever is to its advantage, and we are greatly taken with
every dignity and preeminence! To those who flatter us we
say: "Oh, it is true that I have been gifted with that grace.

Yes, I have it. But it is God's gift. It is a result of His mercy," and other such words. An unimportant gentleman will imagine himself to be from a great family, a cavalier; when someone asks him, "Who are you?" he will answer what he imagines to be the case: "I am a gallant lord, a valiant cavalier, from a great house and family." Ordinarily these men are nobodies. But the less they are, the greater they desire to appear! Folly and nonsense! Who is he? Indeed, who is he? To hear him, he is a St. Peter! He probably lived four hundred years before this apostle, and other such nonsense. In short, our self-love is such that it not only draws to itself all the glory that in any way belongs to it but also that which in no way belongs to it. In this we act quite differently from the glorious St. John, who is not content simply to reject what does not belong to him; he even refuses what he could justly have accepted.

The envoys demand of him: "Since you are not the Christ, are you Elias?" And he declares: "No, I am not." Surely he could have answered that he was; for although he was not Elias in person, he did come, nevertheless, in the spirit of Elias [*Lk.* 1:17; cf. *Matt* 11:14]; so that he could have said of himself as we say today: "He has the spirit of such a one," or, "He does such a thing, impelled by such a spirit."

How, then, if St. John came in the spirit of Elias, can he say in truth that he is not? And he does not lie any more than if he had said that he was Elias. He knew that it was written [*Mal.* 4:5(3:23)] that before the day of the Lord a great prophet, an excellent man named Elias, would rise up among the people, that he would come to teach them and dispose them for the coming of the sovereign Judge. He knew, then, that if he said he was Elias, they would likely take him also for the promised Messias. This is why he denied and said: "I am not." Admirable humility! He rejects not only what does not belong to him (it is the first degree of humility not to wish to admit nor seek to be held or esteemed for what we are not), but he goes much further and finds a manner of speaking by which he can even reject the honor that belongs to him without being untruthful. He does this promptly, without disputing or using many words. Frankly and freely he says: "No, I am not." But I must end this part, for time is passing.

Hearing this second denial, they then asked him a third question: "If you are neither the Christ nor Elias, at least you are some great prophet. You cannot deny this truth, for your works are proof of it and give ample evidence and testimony." Nevertheless, this glorious saint remains firm in his humility and replies: "I am not." But how can St. John in truth make this third denial, he who was not only a prophet but more than a prophet? Our Lord Himself, with His own mouth, declared this aloud to the Jewish people. [*Matt.* 11:9; *Lk.* 1:76; 7:26,28]. How, then, dare he affirm: "I am not." All the ancient Fathers greatly admire these three denials of this glorious saint and are astonished at them. They say that in them St. John went to the furthest extreme, and that if he had gone just a little further, he would have lied. Yet, of course, he did not lie.

But how could he assert that he was not a prophet, knowing indeed that he was and that God Himself had declared it? Note that it was further promised in the Jewish Law [*Deut.* 18:15, 18] that a great prophet would be sent to them. I know there are different opinions as to who this great prophet would be, but the most common is that it would be none other than the Son of God. St. John knew that they were not simply asking him if he were just another prophet, that if he answered affirmatively they would certainly conclude that he was that great promised prophet and acknowledge him as such. So he simply denied it, seeing that without lying he could still answer that he was not. It is as if he said: "If you were only asking me who I am, I would answer you quite simply. If you wanted to know, for instance, if I am merely a prophet, I would frankly admit that I am and even that I was sent to prepare the way for the Messias. [*Lk.* 1:76]. But because all your demands seem to have but the one end, to identify me with the promised Messias, I answer that I am neither the Christ, nor Elias, nor the Prophet." And in this he did not lie.

Notice, then, how St. John eschewed the temptation to pride and ambition and how humility suggested to him skillful ways of not having to admit or accept the honor they wished to render him, cleverly concealing who he really was. He had no doubt that in a figurative sense he was indeed Elias and the Prophet; God Himself had even declared him to be more than a prophet. Nevertheless, seeing that he could truly affirm that he was not as they thought and could thereby avoid the honor they wished to render him—an honor that should be referred to God alone—he answered: "I am not." Without doubt, theologians assure us, we too can speak with a similar skill and prudent cleverness when such is warranted by the circumstances, and this without fear of lying.[7]

But many have interpreted this permission incorrectly and have actually said things far from true without thinking they were lying! Some have even gone so far as to believe that they can utter falsehoods where there is a question of God's glory! If we reprove them for it, saying: "But in such an act or manner of speaking you are untruthful," they will answer, "Oh, that is true, but it is for God's honor that I lied." What utter folly! You are making fun of people by speaking in that way, as if God could actually be honored by a sin! That can never be. We must never lie to honor God. Such is an insult and a great mistake. St. John does not act in that way at all, for he could truthfully answer as he did, as I have just pointed out to you.

Astonished by St. John's denials, these ambassadors retorted: "Why do you baptize if you are not the Christ, nor Elias, nor the Prophet?" [*Jn.* 1:25]. "Why do you have disciples and perform such wonderful deeds? In what spirit do you do these things? Surely, you are trying in vain to hide and conceal. Your works prove to us that you are someone very great indeed. We ask you this so that we may know how to reply to those who sent us." See, they almost lost patience over St. John's humility. (Truly, the ambassadors needed the

great virtue of patience. It is very necessary not only for
ambassadors, but for all Christians. That is why I always
say that patience is the true virtue of Christians.)

"He confessed and did not deny" that he was not the Christ
nor Elias nor the Prophet. These words are better explained
in Hebrew. (The Hebrew language is a marvel, altogether
divine. It is the language Our Lord spoke when He was in
this world, and according to some Doctors' interpretation of
1 Cor. 13:8, it is that which the blessed speak in Heaven
above. Hebrew words always have a remarkable grace in all
they express.) "He confessed and did not deny." These words
are almost identical, because to confess one's fault is not
to deny it; and not to deny it is to confess it. Nevertheless,
there is a slight difference between the two.

On this subject I will say a few words about confession,
although I have touched upon it at other times and in other
churches. But perhaps those who heard me then are not present, and others, I know, have since died.

Many confess and deny at the same time. By this I mean
that many confess their faults, but in such a way that at the
same time that they accuse themselves they excuse themselves.
They admit that if indeed they committed the fault which
they now acknowledge, they certainly had reason for doing
so. Not only do they excuse themselves while accusing themselves, but they accuse others as well. "I became angry and
consequently committed such a failing, but I had good reason for it; they made me do or say such a thing; it was
for such a reason." Is it not clear that in confessing in this
way one is denying it at the same time? Say simply: "It was
through my malice, my impatience and ill nature, or the result of my passions and unmortified inclinations that I committed such and such a fault." Do not say: "I have spoken
ill of others, but it was on matters so obvious that I am not
the only one who said or saw it." By this kind of talk we
deny being guilty of the fault of which we accuse ourselves!

We must not do that. Rather, we must confess clearly and
plainly, owning the fault and holding ourselves truly guilty,

without being anxious about what others may say or think about us. "This is what I am," we ought to say. This is how the glorious St. John acted: "He confessed and did not deny." Without worrying about what others would say or think of him, he walked with determination before God, not like those who go and do not go. We say to some: "You must do this, you must go there." But before doing it or going to the designated place, they make a thousand reflections and hesitations. They are like those servants who, when sent on some errand, do go where they are sent, but they amuse themselves en route at each shop they pass, talking now to this one and now to that one. The least little thing they see stops them. Such people go, while in a sense they are not going.

These ambassadors, then, want to know who St. John is in order to report to those who sent them. But he says nothing to them except: "I am the voice of Him who cries out in the desert: 'Make straight the way of the Lord!' " [*Jn.* 1:22-23; *Is.* 40:3]. Please note this glorious saint's perfect humility. The more they pursue him, the more he withdraws and lowers himself in his nothingness, always rising thereby to a higher degree of humility. O noble virtue of humility! How necessary it is to us on this wicked earth! Not without reason is it called the foundation of all virtues. Without it, there is none. It may not be the preeminent virtue—charity or love of God surpasses it in dignity and excellence—yet these two virtues have such mutual affinity that one is never found without the other.[8]

Since it is to the point, I will relate to you a beautiful sketch on this subject which I read with pleasure in the recently published Lives of the Fathers. The author has gathered these lives diligently and carefully. He relates that many of these good religious had at one point assembled and were talking together familiarly in a spiritual conference. One of them was highly praising obedience; another, charity; a third, patience. Hearing what all his brothers said about these virtues, one of them added; "As for myself, it seems that humility is the first and most necessary of all." He made the following comparison which is my sermon here: "Humility and charity are united like John the Baptist and Our Lord. Humility is the forerunner and the precursor of charity, as St. John the Baptist was of the Saviour. It prepares the way; it is the voice crying out: 'Make straight the way of the Lord.' And just as John the Baptist went before the Messias, so also must humility come in order to empty hearts that they might then receive charity, for that can never dwell in a soul in which humility has not first prepared the lodging for it."

One day St. Anthony was rapt in ecstasy. When he returned to himself, his good confreres asked him what he had seen. He said to them: "I saw the world filled with snares calculated not only to make us stumble, but also to cause us to fall headlong over deep precipices." They replied: "And if it is filled with snares, who then can escape?" He answered them: "Only those who are humble." We see here just how necessary humility is to resist temptations and escape the devil's snares.

St. John had it to a very high degree of perfection. "You ask me why I baptize," he says [*Matt.* 3:11; *Jn.* 1:26]. "I baptize you with water unto penitence; but there is One among you whom you do not recognize, who by baptizing remits sins. You want to know who I am. I tell you that I am nothing but a voice." It is as if he meant to say: "O poor men, how greatly are you deceived in me! You think I am the Messias because I am not dressed like other men, my garment being made of camel's hair. I do not eat bread or meat, and I sustain myself on only locusts and wild honey [*Matt.* 3:4] that the little bees bring me. I drink no wine. [*Lk.* 1:15]. I have no house, but live in the desert with dumb animals. I am on the River Jordan baptizing with water and preaching penitence. [*Lk.* 3:3]. Because of this you believe that I am the Messias. Now I tell you I am not He, but only the voice of Him who cries in the desert." We will continue this next Sunday. We are overtime now.

In declaring that he was only a voice, how could St. John humble himself more? For the voice is only a breath, an exhalation into the air which produces some little sound and then disappears entirely. "You believe that I am the Messias, and I insist that I am not even a man, but only a simple voice. If you go into this desert, you will hear echoes among these rocks; and if you speak, they will answer in an utterance similar to your own. Now who among you will confuse the echo with the person? No one. Well, this is what I am and nothing more." In this way the glorious St. John humbled himself to the very depths of his nothingness. To the same degree that he lowers himself, God exalts him and cries aloud that he is a prophet and more than a prophet.[9] [*Matt.* 11:9; *Lk.* 1:76; 7:26, 28]. Furthermore, He calls him an angel, saying: "Lo, I send my angel to prepare your way before you."[10] [*Mal.* 3:1; cf. *Matt.* 11:10].

Surely from time immemorial Divine Wisdom has looked favorably upon the humble. [*Ps.* 112(113):7; 137(138):6]. He has humbled those who exalted themselves and raised up those who humbled themselves. Our Lady and Mother, your glorious Mistress, has sung of this in her divine canticle: He has put down the mighty from their thrones and exalted the humble. [*Lk.* 1:52]. Everyone who exalts himself shall be humbled. Those who wish to place their throne upon the clouds will be brought down, and the poor who lower and humble themselves shall be exalted. [*1 Kgs.(1 Sam.)* 2:7-8; *Matt.* 23:12; *Lk.* 14:11; 18:14].

There are some people so full of pride that they cannot subject themselves to anyone or suffer anyone to say what they really are. They want to be preferred to everyone, and they esteem themselves more learned and erudite than any other, and it seems to them they never need a teacher. Actually, such people are usually extremely ignorant, but no one dares to tell them that, for they suppose themselves to be veritable marvels. Oh, God humbles such as these. He leaves them and looks upon the poor and humble souls who are prostrate and have no throne but their littleness. [*Ps.* 112 (113):6-7; *Lk.* 1:48, 52]. These are not offended when we tell them that they are imprudent and have no sense or judgment. They humble themselves, and God exalts and raises them up, giving them His Spirit by which they perform great things.

In short, Our Lord offers St. John to all kinds of people for their imitation. He should be the model not only of prelates and preachers, but also of religious men and women. They should consider his humility and mortification so that, in following his example, they also may be voices crying out that we should prepare the way and make straight the path of the Lord so that, receiving Him in this life, we may enjoy Him in the next, to which may the Father, the Son and the Holy Spirit lead us all. Amen.

NOTES

1. Cf. Note 3 below. Cf. also *Sermons of St. Francis de Sales on Our Lady* (Rockford, Ill.: TAN Books and Publishers, Inc., 1985), "The Purification," February 2, 1622, pp. 179-180. In subsequent notes this work will be referred to as *Sermons on Our Lady.*
2. Cf. *Sermons on Our Lady,* "The Purification," February 2, 1620, p. 88; *Sermons of St. Francis de Sales for Lent* (Rockford, Ill.: TAN Books and Publishers, Inc., 1987), "Hearing the Word of God," Passion Sunday, March 13, 1622, p. 153. In subsequent notes this work will be referred to as *Sermons for Lent.*
3. The "heaven" from which Lucifer fell was not the Heaven of glory and the Beatific Vision but was rather the abode of the angels during their period of probation; no sin is possible in the abode of the blessed.
4. Cf. *Sermons on Our Lady,* "The Visitation," July 2, 1618, p. 51.
5. Cf. *Sermons on Our Lady,* "The Visitation," July 2, 1618, p. 51.
6. Cf. *Sermons on Our Lady,* "The Annunciation," March 25, 1621, p. 136.
7. Cf. St. Francis de Sales: *Introduction to the Devout Life,* Part III, chap. 30.
8. *Spiritual Conferences,* VIII, "On Self-Renouncement," p. 136.
9. Cf. p. 28 of this sermon.
10. St. John the Baptist can be called an angel because "angel" means "messenger."

— 3 —

PENITENCE

Sermon for the Fourth Sunday of Advent, December 20, 1620, concerning St. John the Baptist as the voice of Our Lord and his obligation to proclaim His word, the corresponding obligation of hearers to listen to and profit by God's word, procrastination and spiritual avarice as reasons why we fail to profit from God's word, two meanings of Isaias' words: Because your malice and wickedness have reached their height, your sins shall be forgiven; the very surprising ways of God's mercy, how cooperation with a grace brings subsequent graces, the Incarnation's occurrence at the height of men's wickedness, God's forgiveness of St. Paul and David and others at the height of their malice, the penitence indicated by St. John's exhortations to prepare the way of the Lord: tempering fear with confidence, getting rid of presumption and pride, straightening our intentions, seeking opportunities for penitence, and acquiring an even disposition by mortifying our passions, inclinations and aversions, thus evening out the way for our Saviour's coming.

> *"The word of the Lord came to John, the son of Zachary, in the desert. And he came into all the country about the Jordan, preaching the baptism of penance for the remission of sins."*
> —*Lk.* 3:2-3

As I pointed out last Sunday, when he was questioned as to whether he was the Christ, or Elias, or the Prophet, the glorious St. John testified abundantly and gave excellent proof

35

of his humility. St. John knew that when Moses spoke of Our Lord's coming he indicated that a great Prophet would first come before Him. [*Deut.* 18:15, 18]. He also realized that the Jews thought that he was the one who had been promised. Therefore, he openly avowed: *Non sum,* "I am not He!" Great humility indeed—and no one expressed that humility better than St. John the Evangelist when he wrote: He confessed and did not deny that he was not the Christ. [*Jn.* 1:19-23]. But when they pressed him to say who he was so that they might inform those who had sent them, he replied: I am the voice of Him who cries in the desert: Make straight the way of the Lord.

It is as if he meant: "Do you wish to know who I am? I am only the voice of Him who cries out in the desert, that is, I am not He who cries, but only His voice." It was not St. John who cried out, but Our Lord through the mouth of St. John. That is what the great Apostle St. Paul said to the Corinthians. "Do you think," he wrote to them, "that it is I who speak to you? Oh no, rather it is God who speaks through my mouth. Do not receive my words as human words, but as divine words, for I tell you in truth that it is not I who teach but God through me." [*2 Cor.* 5:20; cf. *1 Thess.* 2:13].

Now St. John was by the River Jordan, at the edge of the desert, crying out and preaching penitence.[1] [*Lk.* 3:3]. People hastened from all sides to hear him and to be baptized by him. It was there that he cried out: "Do penance! Prepare the way, make straight the paths, for the Lord is near. [*Matt.* 3:1-3, 5-6; *Mk.* 1:4-5]. But because I cry out and preach in the desert, you want to know who I am. I protest to you that I am only the voice of Him who cries out. It is not I who cry out in the desert: 'Do penance.' It is God who says it to you through me, and I am only the voice, the trumpet He uses so that you will understand how you are to prepare to do penance and dispose yourselves for His coming. That is what I am. And you ought to hear my words, not as mine, but as those of God who speaks to you through my mouth, for I am the voice of Him who cries out in the desert." We will dwell on this point.[2]

St. John was the son of Zachary [*Lk.* 3:2], and the word of God came to him not merely that he might treasure it within himself, but that he might also communicate it to others. The divine word comes into a heart in two ways: first, when Our Lord speaks to it to instruct and enlighten it concerning His will and good pleasure, making known what is necessary for its guidance and its own individual concerns. The second is when it comes into the heart not for itself alone, but that it may also be carried and communicated to others so that they might know the divine will.

Our text, then, "The word of the Lord came to the son of Zachary," must be understood in both these ways. First, St. John was chosen and elected by God to be His voice, His herald. Note here (I say it in passing) that no one can be received to Orders or the episcopate unless the sacred word has come to him, that is, unless he is chosen and elected by God. Now this choice or election is commonplace and normal, and we ought neither to desire nor to seek special and extraordinary callings; actually, such extraordinary callings are dangerous and suspect when they have not been authenticated and confirmed by pastors and masters of the spiritual life.[3] As for St. John, he was chosen and elected by God, who Himself authenticated his calling and manner of proceeding. He sent him before Him [*Lk.* 1:17, 76], and He came after him, preaching what John had preached. [*Matt.* 3:2; 4:17].

In the second place, this word signified that the Lord had given him a ministry in which he must labor for others, announcing to them the necessity of penitence. From all this we are taught that when God bestows some responsibility upon those whom He has chosen for His service, as upon preachers, they must apply themselves to their duty diligently, and communicate to others what they have received and what God has given them for this purpose. It is in this sense that we ought to understand these words of the Gospel. The word

of the Lord came to John, the son of Zachary, who was chosen by Divine Wisdom to be the precursor of our Divine
Saviour. He ought to proclaim His word, preach penitence
and perform the functions of his office.

He was bound to cry out that the people must prepare the
way and that they must level the paths and roads of the Lord.
The people whom he addressed were likewise bound to listen, to receive the baptism he offered them, and to do what
he told them. If the preacher has the duty to preach to you,
you also have that of listening to him and of receiving with
good dispositions what he announces to you on behalf of
God. I come here to preach to you, but if I am bound to
bring the divine word to you, you are bound to pay attention
to it, and not only that but to learn it well and carry out
what you are taught. For this you must indeed masticate well
what is heard and garnered, and endeavor to digest it well.
For of what good would it have been to the Israelites for
God to have sent them manna in the desert for their nourish-
ment if they had not been willing to gather and collect it,
if they had not been willing to eat it so that it might become
part of their own substance? Surely when Divine Providence
let the manna fall from Heaven, it obliged the children of
Israel to rise in the morning to collect it before the sun rose
on the horizon [*Ex.* 16:21; *Wis.* 16:28]; and not only that,
but also to eat and swallow it in order to be nourished and
strengthened. Likewise, those who hear God's word are duty
bound to keep it and profit by it.

There are two reasons why people do not profit by the
word of God. The first is that, though they may indeed hear
it and be interiorly moved by it, they postpone its accomplishment until tomorrow. Alas, we poor creatures do not
realize that this procrastination is the cause of our death and
destruction and that our good is found in the present moment, which is today. Our life is the today in which we are
living; who can promise himself a tomorrow? [*Jas.* 4:13-15].
Absolutely no one—no matter who he is. Our life consists
in *today,* in this present moment in which we are living,

and we cannot promise or assure ourselves of any other than that which we now enjoy, however brief that may be. Now if this is so, how dare we put off doing what we have heard to be useful for our conversion, since our whole life really depends on each present moment when we hear what must be done. This is the first reason why we often do not profit from what is said and taught to us.

The second reason is "spiritual avarice,"[4] by which we seek to obtain a great deal of knowledge and to amass a huge stock of devotional exercises. You will find some people who never tire of amassing new writings and instructions, all sorts of spiritual advice and information, and who nevertheless do not put any of it into practice![5] And what is that if not spiritual avarice, a truly serious fault in the devout life? You will find others who must always be hearing and seeing something new. To attract attention they collect innumerable books and create libraries that are wonders to behold. "Poor creatures, what is the purpose in all that?" They will respond: "Oh, we are practicing foresight in anticipating our future needs. When older, we can make good use of them." "O God! do you not realize that Our Lord strongly desired to remove such avarice and anxiety from His disciples' hearts and commanded them to live from hand to mouth and to have no anxiety about tomorrow"? [*Matt.* 6:34].

Indeed, among the ordinances which God imposed on the children of Israel was the command to collect only a certain measure of manna [*Ex.* 16:16], that is, only what was necessary for each one's daily portion. Furthermore, He commanded that no one should store any for the morrow, that no one should gather more than was specified in an attempt to make provision, for it would breed worms and rot. [*Ex.* 16:19-20]. Live each day well, eat what is given you, and you will nourish yourself well by putting that into practice. Leave the rest to Divine Providence, which will surely provide sufficiently for your needs. Use well only what is given you, and be free of all other care.

It is a fact that meats which are stored breed worms, and

I believe that the worms that torment the consciences of the damned [*Is.* 66:24; *Mk.* 9:45, 47(48)] are not the least, but the greatest pain they endure. And what are these worms if not the active and biting pangs of remorse of conscience which sting and torment the soul at the vivid remembrance of so many means and opportunities they had of serving God. What remorse of conscience will they feel at death, seeing the numerous writings, advice and instructions they had received for their perfection. These will be the cause of their greatest pain. So spiritual avarice is the second reason why we fail to profit from God's word.

Let this be said only by way of introduction to my sermon. Let us return to our Gospel. [*Lk.* 3:1-6]. I shall explain it to you as simply as possible; but to do so I must briefly relate the account. At the time that Tiberius Caesar was emperor, Herod was tetrarch of Galilee, Pontius Pilate was presiding in Jerusalem, and Annas and Caiphas were high priests and sitting in the chair of Moses [*Lk.* 3:1-2; *Matt.* 23:2], God sent His prophet who was His voice that cried in the desert: "Make straight the way of the Lord, do penance, for salvation is at hand." We shall take as an explanation of these words those which Isaias spoke to the Israelites in chapter 40 of his prophecies. [*Is.* 40:1-4]. These verses are among the most comforting and pleasing that can be heard. It is truly a delight to read the writings of that holy prophet; his words are a river of honey, overflowing with incomparable wisdom. From his very first chapter we find a remarkable style. Surely he is a river and torrent of eloquence.

The people of Israel had been led forth into captivity by the Gentiles and sent as prisoners among the Medes and Persians. After their long captivity, the good Cyrus decided to free them from that slavery and lead them back to the Promised Land. Foreseeing this, the prophet Isaias wrote these beautiful and heavenly poetic words: "*Consolamini, consolamini*: O people of Israel, be consoled and comforted. Again I tell you, be consoled and comforted. Let these words console you: Because your malice and wickedness have reached their height, your sins shall be forgiven. Therefore, make level your ways and straight your roads, so that Cyrus may find no rough ways while leading the people back to the Promised Land."

There are a great many interpretations of this text: "Because they have reached the height of their malice, their sins shall be forgiven." What does he mean? Why does the Prophet say that God will pardon the people of Israel because they have reached the height of their malice?

This is how the ancient Fathers say that these words should be understood: When they had reached the limit of their labors and sufferings and had, in slavery and bondage, come to a greater sense of their iniquities; when they had been punished enough for their wickedness by such tribulation; then I, the Lord, cast My compassionate eyes upon them. At the height of their malice, during the worst of their days, I was satisfied that they had suffered enough for their sins, and therefore I determined that their sins shall be forgiven. Anticipating this period of great suffering, Jacob cried out: My days, though short, are full of affliction. [*Gen.* 47:9]. By this he meant: "Life is short, only a passing shadow, soon gone. [*Job.* 8:9; 14:2; *Ps.* 101(102):12; 143(144):4], yet it is full of affliction, overburdened with the many labors that accompany it. Though short, it is always full of evils." He spoke in this way because of the great labors and tribulations his people were going to endure in exile.

Here is another way of understanding these words, "Because their malice has reached its height, their sins shall be forgiven." When they have reached the height, the noontide, the high point of their wickedness and ingratitude, and when all memory of God and His benefits is gone, then their sins shall be forgiven; that is, at that very moment when they deserve to be cast aside, God will pardon them and will no longer remember their wickedness.

Certainly whenever Divine Providence revealed the greatness of His mercy in the past it was always in the most surprising ways. When there was nothing to hope for but the fury of His wrath and the terror of His Justice; when there was absolutely no human merit or good on which to hope for the Lord's mercy, it was precisely then that He let His awe-inspiring deeds on their behalf shine forth.

Indeed, these are examples of God's great goodness to the human family: to bestow His graces upon His creatures, to pardon continually their daily faults against Him, and to reward their slightest services with the greatest favors. According to the most true teaching of theology, the one who cooperates with God's first grace disposes himself to receive the second, and by cooperating with the second he is prepared to obtain the third, and then the fourth, and so on consecutively. Theologians teach that God's grace is never lacking to us[6] and that if we are faithful in cooperating with the first grace, we are disposed to receive the second, third and fourth, and in this way to come to participate in the highest benefits and obtain most special favors.[7] For this reason, in many places in Holy Scripture God recommends to us fidelity in following good impulses, lights and inspirations. In such the greatness of His mercy surely shines forth.

But when, over and above this, His Providence wanted to make an even more glorious revelation of His mercy, it was by a most wonderful deed, one in which He willed that no exterior motive should induce Him to act. Urged solely by His goodness, He communicated Himself in a wholly marvelous way when He came into this world. The Incarnation took place at a time when men were at the height of their wickedness: when the Jews were without king and the laws were in the hands of Annas and Caiphas, wicked men; when Herod reigned and Pontius Pilate was governor; when there were no worthy priests [Cf. *Matt.* 9:36], when both priests and people constituted an evil generation. In short, when the world had reached the high point of its wickedness, God came to redeem us and deliver us from the tyranny of sin and the servitude of our enemies. Urged to it solely by His immense goodness, He became incarnate for us.

Certainly, the Heart of our dear Saviour and Master was

wholly filled with mercy and kindness for the human family. [*Lk.* 1:78]. In this one act He gave abundant witness to it, as He did on many other occasions in which His clemency shone forth in its beauty and grandeur. When did He pardon St. Paul? When he was at the height of his malice his sins were forgiven him; for everyone knows that at the time of his conversion this Apostle was in the throes of his greatest hatred and fury against Jesus Christ. Not able to vent his rage against Jesus Himself, he directed his wrath against His Church, but with such fury that he foamed with rage like one insane, a madman totally beside himself. [*Acts* 8:3; 9:1; *Gal.* 1:13]. It was precisely at that point that Our Lord countered his malice and ingratitude with His meekness and infinite mercy, touching him and pardoning all his iniquities—at the very moment in which he had completely forfeited such mercy. [*Acts* 9:3-7; *1 Cor.* 15:9]. O God, how vast were the riches of Your goodness toward that Apostle!

Nevertheless, we see similar instances of this goodness every day. When sinners are most hardened in their sins, when they have reached the point of living as if there were no God, no Heaven or Hell, it is often then that the Lord allows them to find His Heart full of pity and kind mercy toward them. I never read of David's conversion without trembling in awe at how he committed such grave sins and remained an entire year in sin without acknowledging the fact, as if he were asleep, with no recognition of his terrible crime before God.[8] [*2 Kgs.*(*2 Sam.*) 11; 12:1-14]. Perhaps there might have been some excuse for him if he had sinned while still a shepherd tending his sheep. But David grievously offended God after having received very special graces and many inspirations, lights and favors. God had made him a man after His own Heart [*1 Kgs.*(*1 Sam.*) 13:14] and allowed him to perform many marvels and prodigies. David had always been nourished in the Heart of sweet clemency and divine mercy; and the fact that despite such great favors he should have committed such heinous offenses and remained an entire year without acknowledging them—oh, that greatly astounds me.

He began with adultery, but that meant little to him. Is
it not amazing how unwilling the human spirit is to
acknowledge its faults? When guilty of them it tries to conceal
them by committing even more grievous ones! David tried
to get the good Urias drunk. There was more malice in this
sin than in the adultery. But when his plan was unsuccessful,
Urias being an upright man and a brave soldier who could
not be caught by surprise in such a vice, David decided to
commit yet a third fault in order to conceal the first two.
This was even more grievous than the first two, for he decided
to kill him. He ordered his lieutenant to expose Urias to
the enemy and then abandon him. Although the lieutenant
was a just man, he believed himself bound to obey the King's
orders, and he did what he was ordered. This affair so entan-
gled poor David that he committed countless other sins, pil-
ing one on top of the other and committing the next as a
cover-up for the preceding. He remained an entire year en-
meshed in his iniquity, never calling to mind his God. [Cf.
Ps. 41(42):4].

There he was, without any inclination whatsoever toward
grace. Yet seeing him in this blindness, the Divine Goodness
sent him the prophet Nathan, who asked him what he had
done and where God was in his life. So blind was David
in his own regard that the prophet wisely and subtly brought
him round to confess his crime. He spoke to him of some
fault that one of his subjects had committed, and David passed
this judgment on the crime: "He stole that poor man's sheep.
He must die!" This made it clear just how blind and hardened David had become in his own sin; yet for the faults
of others he knew well how to impose just and proportionate
punishment. Nevertheless, God did not abandon him in that
condition, but used the prophet Nathan to make him confess
his crime.

What greater evidence of divine mercy could one desire,
for when David was at the height of his malice, God pardoned
his iniquities? But what a transformation this conversion
resulted in. Acknowledging his fault, this great king kept

lamenting and deploring his blindness. He kept repeating, *Peccavi,* "I have sinned," and kept crying out for mercy to the Lord, endlessly repeating, *Miserere mei, Deus,* "Have mercy on me, O God." [*Ps.* 50(51):3; 55(56):2]. There are hundreds of similar examples in Holy Scripture, examples in which God showed the same kind of mercy. We should therefore understand Isaias' words in this way.

The following words of Isaias: "Prepare the way, make straight the paths," had originally been said in reference to the great Cyrus and his delivery of the Israelites from captivity into the Promised Land. Yet the Prophet's principal object in these words was to speak of Our Lord's coming. Accordingly, St. John made use of these very words, preaching penitence and announcing to the people that the Saviour was near. "I am," he said, "the voice of Him who cries out in the desert: Make straight the way of the Lord." Since the Lord is near [*Phil.* 4:5], how are we to prepare for His coming? St. John tells us when he says: Do penance, for the Lord is near. Most certainly penitence is the best disposition for the Saviour's coming; since we are all sinners, we must all take the path of penitence. But we are now speaking too much in generalities. Let us treat of some particulars in this matter.

St. John gives some particulars in today's Gospel. Make straight the way of the Lord, fill up the valleys, lower the mountains and hills. They, as well as the ditches and valleys, trouble travelers. Make straight the paths. Those that twist and turn fatigue the pilgrim greatly. Our life too contains many hills, valleys and tortuous ways which can be put right only by penitence. Penitence fills up the valleys, lays low the mountains, makes straight and smoothes the ways. Do penance, says St. John; lower those mountains of pride, fill up those valleys, those ditches of lukewarmness and tepidity.

The valleys which the glorious St. John wants us to fill up are none other than fear which, when it is excessive, leads to discouragement at the sight of our sins. Fill up the valleys; that is, fill your heart with confidence and hope because

salvation is near at hand. [*Lk.* 21:28; *Rom.* 13:11]. The sight
of our great faults brings with it a certain horror and shock,
a certain fear and terror which unnerves the heart and often
leads it to discouragement. These are the ditches and valleys
that must be filled up for Our Lord's coming.

One day the good St. Thais (I must tell you this because
it comes to my mind and is apropos) said this to St. Paphnutius: "Father, what am I to do? The memory of my miserable life terrifies me." She had been a great sinner, and was
now filled with fear because of those past sins. The good
saint replied: "Take care not to raise your eyes to Heaven,
you who have time and again used them to cast dangerous
glances, to flirt, and the like. And do not raise those hands
through which you have performed so many evil deeds.
Throughout your whole life, exercise yourself in humility and
confide yourself to the goodness of God. Fear, but hope at
the same time. Fear lest you become haughty and proud,
hope lest you fall into discouragement and despair." Fear and
hope ought never to be without one another, since fear without hope is despair and hope without fear is presumption.
We must, then, fill up these valleys formed by the fear which
comes from the knowledge of the great imperfections and
sins we have committed. We must fill them with confidence
mingled with the fear of God.

Lower the mountains and hills. What are these mountains
but presumption and pride, which are very great obstacles
to Our Lord's coming? He humbles and lowers the haughty
[*Matt.* 23:12; *Lk.* 1:52; 18:14] and penetrates the depths of
the heart to discover the pride that lies hidden there. It is
useless to say to Him: "I am a bishop, a priest, a religious."[9]
Well and good; but if you are a bishop, how do you conduct
yourself in this ministry? What is your life like; are your
morals congruent with your vocation? Are you full of arrogance and presumption like the Pharisee in the Gospel
[*Lk.* 18:10-14], or are you like the humble publican?

The Pharisee was a mountain of pride. True, he possessed
some outward semblance of virtue, but he boasted and gloried

in it. He said boldly: I give You thanks, O God, that I am not like the rest of men; I pay tithes, I fast so many times a week, and so on. Seeing his pride, God rejected him. And that poor publican, who in the sight of the world was a high and rugged mountain, was lowered and made smooth in the sight of the Divine Majesty when he came to the Temple. Not daring to raise his eyes to Heaven because of his great sins, he remained at the entrance with a contrite and humble heart. As a result he was worthy of finding grace before God. I could still say many more things on this subject, but I shall be content for now with what I have already touched upon.

The glorious St. John adds: Make ready the ways, that is, repair those that are tortuous, make them straight and even. Roads that twist and turn too much only weary and mislead travelers. We must make them straight and even for Our Lord's coming. We must correct so many perverse and devious intentions and have only one, that of pleasing God by doing penance. This must be the only goal to which we aspire. We ought to be like the mariner who, in steering his vessel, always keeps his eye on the needle of the compass; and those who sail their little boats always keep their hands on the tiller.

We too must always have our eyes open to opportunities for penitence. Some people are unwilling to do penance until they are no longer able to take advantage of it. "Oh," they say, "God is so good and merciful, we can settle affairs with Him later on; let us enjoy ourselves now. At the hour of death we will say a fervent 'I have sinned' [2 *Kgs.* (2 *Sam.*) 12:13] and God will pardon us." Is it not great presumption on their part to take advantage of the Divine Goodness by continuing to live in their sins? They do not realize that although God is infinitely merciful, He is also infinitely just. When His mercy is thus presumed, it provokes His justice. [Cf. *Rom.* 2:4-5].

Make straight the way of the Lord, that is, acquire an even disposition by the mortification of your passions, inclinations and aversions. An even disposition is the most pleasing virtue in the spiritual life, one for which we must work continually.[10] My God, how utterly delightful it is to reflect upon the life of our dear Saviour and Master. There we find this perfect equanimity of spirit shining brilliantly in the midst of all sorts of changing circumstances. Certainly, no one but He and the sacred and sinless Virgin enjoyed it to such perfection. All the other saints labored diligently to acquire it and, to a degree, have done so—but none perfectly. In each of them something marred the perfection of their equanimity of spirit. This was true even for St. John the Baptist, for according to some Doctors he had sinned venially.[11]

O God, how pleasing it is to find this even disposition in someone. Most of us are far from it, so changing and inconstant. There are some people who, when in a happy mood, maintain a pleasant conversation. But before we can turn around, they are disturbed and troubled. There are others we can speak to at this moment in a certain way, but within an hour we must use a totally different approach. A certain person will just now have been sweet and lighthearted, but in a little bit he will be harsh and bitter. Indeed, all we find among us are capriciousness and fickleness.

These are the *ways* we should even out for our Saviour's coming. To do this well, we must go to the school of the glorious St. John the Baptist and place ourselves, or rather ask him to receive us, among his disciples. For do you not see that this great saint sent his disciples to the Saviour to be instructed by Him personally; he entrusted them into His hands, and our Saviour kept them. After St. John's death they became His disciples. If this glorious precursor receives us, he will surely place us in the hands of our Saviour, who in turn will place us in the hands of the Eternal Father, whom we shall praise for all eternity together with Him and the Holy Spirit. Amen.

NOTES

1. Throughout this sermon, St. Francis uses the French *pénitence* and *faites pénitence*; these have been translated "penitence" and "do penance," respectively. In his *Treatise on the Love of God* (Book 2, chap. 18), St. Francis explains what he means when he uses the word *pénitence*—it includes reparation: "To use general terms, penitence is a form of repentance in which a man rejects and detests the sin he has committed, together with a resolution to repair in so far as he can the offense and injury done to him against whom he sinned. In penitence I include the purpose of repairing the offense, since repentance that willingly permits its chief effect, viz., the offense and injury, to remain does not sufficiently detest the evil committed. Moreover, as long as such repentance can repair the injury in some way but does not do so, it permits the injury to exist."

2. Cf. p. 32 of this volume.

3. Cf. *Controversies*, Part I, chap. 1, art. 3; *Treatise on the Love of God*, Book 8, chap. 13.

4. Cf. *Sermons for Lent*, "Temptation," First Sunday of Lent, February 13, 1622, pp. 29-30; "Election and Reprobation," Thursday of Second Week, February 24, 1622, pp. 73-74; *Spiritual Conferences*, XII, "Simplicity and Religious Prudence," pp. 214-215; XIII, "The Spirit of the Rules," p. 247.

5. Cf. *Spiritual Conferences*, VII, "Three Spiritual Laws," p. 111.

6. Cf. St. Francis de Sales: *Treatise on the Love of God*, Book 4, chap. 5.

7. St. Francis de Sales is speaking here on one of his favorite topics: God's grace and our free cooperation with it. God's grace is always prior to our cooperation with it, but it comes to us as an enabling and inviting grace, one that brings about our free cooperation with it. See St. Francis' *Treatise on the Love of God*, Book 4, chap. 5.

8. Cf. *Sermons for Lent*, "Temptation," First Sunday of Lent, February 13, 1622, p. 16.

9. Cf. pp. 10, 18 of this volume.

10. Cf. pp. 16-17 of this volume.

11. Cf. *Sermons on Our Lady*, "The Assumption," August 15, 1602, p. 17; "The Visitation," July 2, 1618, p. 51.

4

THE COMING OF
THE DIVINE INFANT

Sermon for Christmas Eve, December 24, 1613, concerning vigils, the manna in the desert, the mystery of the Incarnation, Our Lady as Star of the Sea and Morning Star and how she produced Our Lord virginally as stars produce light, the three tastes of the manna—flour, honey and oil—and what they represent in the Divine Infant: His divine nature, His soul and His body; the shepherds and whom they represent, Our Lord's swaddling clothes—why He was wrapped in them and what they teach us, how we should visit and bring a gift to the Divine Infant, the special individual consolation each visitor will receive in return, how our senses and interior faculties are restless and dissipated until they have chosen Our Lord for their king, and how we should always remain near Our Lord.

*Today you will know that the Lord is coming,
and in the morning you will see His glory.*
— Ex. 16:6-7

Holy Church usually prepares us for great solemnities with vigils to help us appreciate more the great benefits we have received from God in the events celebrated. In the primitive Church, the faithful Christians desired to render satisfaction to Our Lord in some way for the Blood He had shed for them in dying on the Cross. Therefore, they very carefully celebrated the time of feasts, solemnizing them to the best of their ability. Because of this desire, there was scarcely any feast without its vigil on which to prepare for the solemnity. This was done not only in the Church but also in the Old Law, where there were many preparations on the day before the Sabbath.

The Church wants us to prepare for the holy day of Christmas with a vigil. Not wanting us to be unprepared for so great a mystery, this loving Mother tells us: "You shall know today that Our Lord will come tomorrow," that is, "He will be born tomorrow, and you will see Him as an Infant laid in a manger." [*Lk.* 2:12]. These words are adapted from those used by Moses to alert the Israelites to the day that God had chosen to give them manna in the desert. He assembled them together and spoke thus to them: In the evening you will know that the Lord brought you out of the land of Egypt, and in the morning you will see the glory of the Lord. [*Ex.* 16:6-7]. It is as if he meant to say: "He will come tomorrow in the morning." He spoke of the Lord's "coming" in glory, although we all know that God does not "go" and "come" like one with a body. He is immutable, firm, solid and without any movement. Nevertheless, Moses spoke in this way to indicate how great a benefit the manna was, suggesting that God Himself had brought and distributed it to the Israelites. Because it was so great a gift, Moses had them carefully prepare themselves by reflecting on this great benefit in an effort to render themselves more worthy to receive it. In this same way the Church says to us: "You will know today that the Lord is coming tomorrow." By this vigil she wants us to ponder deeply on the grandeur of the mystery of the most holy Nativity of Our Lord.

To do this better let us first humble our understanding, realizing that we are totally incapable of exhausting the great depth of this uniquely Christian mystery. It is uniquely Christian inasmuch as only Christianity has ever fathomed how God is man and man is God. Actually, humanity has always had a certain inclination toward believing in something like the possibility of the Incarnation; but only Christianity has, in Jesus, ever come to know how it could be. I believe that

certain Old Testament prophets and some privileged others
knew of it, but the vast majority did not. Among the pagans
this instinct for something like the Incarnation manifested itself
in strange, often bizarre, ways. At least some of them believed that they could make *themselves* gods and be adored
as such by others! For they thought that even if there were
a Supreme God who is the first principle of all things, there
could nevertheless be many lesser gods, or that at least some
men who shared in some way in divine qualities could be
called gods. When Alexander the Great was near death, his
mad, flattering and foolish courtiers asked him, "Sire, when
do you want us to make you a god?" In his reply Alexander
demonstrated clearly that he was not as foolish as they: "You
are to make me a god when you are blessed." By this reply
he meant: "It is not possible for unhappy, perishable and
mortal men to make gods, who by definition are happy and
immortal."

Christians have been more enlightened and have had the
honor of knowing of the Incarnation, that man is God and
God is man,[1] although even they are incapable of completely
penetrating its mystery.

For this is a mystery hidden in the obscurity of night's
darkness. Of course the mystery is not really dark at all,
for God is only light. [*Jn.* 1:5,9; *1 Jn.* 1:5]. Just as our un-
aided eyes cannot look directly into the sun's brilliant light
without our having to close them immediately, being momen-
tarily blinded, so, in a similar way, our understanding is
blinded and darkened by the brilliant light and splendor of
the mystery of the Incarnation. Our understanding, the eye
of our soul, cannot consider this mystery for any length of
time without becoming clouded, humbly confessing that it
cannot penetrate it deeply enough to understand how God
became incarnate in the virginal womb of the most holy Virgin and how He became one like us to make us like God.

God rained manna in the desert night for the children of
Israel. [*Num.* 11:9]. To increase their gratitude to Him, He
Himself arranged the feast and set the table. For Moses said:

"You will know that the Lord brought you out of the land of Egypt, and in the morning you shall see His glory." He first made a sweet dew descend from Heaven to serve as a tablecloth upon the desert. Then the manna fell like little coriander seeds. Finally, to show that He honored them as one now serves princes with covered plates, He made a little dew rain down to preserve the manna until the morning when the Israelites gathered it up before the sunrise. [*Ex.* 16:13-14,21,31; *Num.* 11:7, 9; *Wis.* 16:27-28].

But God desired an even greater and more loving gift for us who live on earth as in a desert, and who long for the joy of the Promised Land, our heavenly country. He came Himself to bring us this gift, and He came in the middle of the night. [*Wis.* 18:14-15]. This special gift is the grace which helps us to attain what would otherwise be impossible for us: the joy and happiness of glory. Thus, in the darkness of the night Our Lord was born and appeared to us as an infant lying in a manger, as we shall see tomorrow.

Reflect a bit on how this happened. The most holy Virgin produced her Son virginally, as the stars produce their light. Now, one of Our Lady's titles is that of "Star of the Sea" or "Morning Star." The star of the sea is the polar star toward which the mariner's needle always points. By it captains navigate on the sea and can discern their direction and course. Everyone knows that the ancient Fathers of the Church, as well as the Patriarchs and Prophets, kept their sights on this polar star, sailing by its favor. Ship captains have always looked to the North Star to avoid the shipwrecks which are so usual in sailing the waters of this miserable world.

The most sacred Virgin is also that morning star [Cf. *Num.* 24:17] which brings us the gracious news of the coming of the true Sun. [*Lk.* 1:78]. All the prophets knew that the Virgin would conceive and bring forth a child [*Is.* 7:14] who would be at once both God and man. She conceived, but by virtue of the Holy Spirit. [*Lk.* 1:35]. She conceived and delivered her Son virginally. Having chosen her for His Mother because of her virginity, is it likely that He would have violated her virginity at His birth? Could Purity Itself in any way diminish His most holy Mother's purity?

Our Lord is begotten virginally from all eternity in the bosom of His Heavenly Father. He shares in the one divinity of His Eternal Father, without dividing it or fracturing the divine simplicity. He remains one same God with Him. The most holy Virgin produced her Son Our Lord on earth as He is produced by His Father eternally in Heaven, that is, virginally. There is one important difference, however; she brought Him forth from her womb and not in her womb, for once He left it He will no more return there, but His Heavenly Father begets Him from His bosom and in His bosom, and He shall remain there eternally.[2]

All this ought not be sifted and examined overly curiously, nor ought we to overtax our understanding in the examination of this divine birth. It is a little too lofty for us. It is good, however, to use it as a foundation for our meditations on the mystery of Our Lord's Nativity.

With this in mind, it is with good reason that the most holy Virgin has a name which signifies star. Stars produce their light virginally and without any detriment to themselves. Quite the contrary, for the light makes them even more beautiful to us. In the same manner Our Lady produced the inaccessible Light [*1 Tim.* 6:16] of her most blessed Son, without receiving any injury from it nor staining in any way her virginal purity. There was, however, this difference. She produced Him without any effort, nor shock, nor any violence whatsoever. This is not the case with the stars, for it is clear that they produce their light by shocks and, it seems, with violence and force.

Let us return to the manna for our second consideration. The manna had three kinds of tastes which were proper and particular to it, besides having every taste [*Wis.* 16:20, 25] that one could desire it to have. If the Israelites wanted to eat bread, the manna had the taste of bread; if they wanted to eat partridge and other such things, the manna had that taste. The majority of the Fathers doubt whether both bad and good Israelites enjoyed this favor. Be that as it may, the manna had the particular taste or flavor of flour, honey and oil. [*Ex.* 16:31; *Num.* 11:8]. These symbolize the three substances which are found in the most blessed Infant, whom we shall see tomorrow lying in the manger. Just as these three tastes were found in one single food, manna, so in the person of Our Lord there are three "substances" which constitute but one same Person who is at once both God and man.

In this most blessed Baby are found the divine nature, the nature of the soul and that of the body.[3] In the manna was the taste of honey, which is actually a heavenly liquid; for although bees gather honey from among flowers, they do not take it from flowers. Rather, they imbibe with their little mouth the honey which falls upon the flowers from Heaven along with the dew, and this only at a certain time of the year.[4] Likewise, at the very moment of His Incarnation, Our Lord's divine nature descended from Heaven onto this blessed flower, the most holy Virgin our Lady, where human nature gathered It and preserved It in the hive of the Virgin's glorious womb for nine months. After that It was placed in the crib, where we shall see It tomorrow.

The taste of oil found in the manna represents the nature of Our Lord's most holy soul. What else is His most blessed soul but an oil, a balm, a spreading perfume [*Cant.* 1:2(3)] whose excellent fragrance infinitely satisfies those who smell it? What fragrance did it not spread forth in the presence of the Divine Majesty, seeing itself in union with It without having done anything to merit it! What acts of perfect charity and profound humility did it not make at this very moment of Incarnation when it entered into a sacred and incomparable union with the Eternal Word! And what incomparably sweet fragrance has it not poured forth so as to move us to follow and imitate its perfections! [*Cant.* 1:3(4)].

Finally, the taste of flour, also found in manna, represents the other aspect of Our Lord's most holy humanity, His adorable body, which, when crushed on the tree of the Cross, was made into a very precious Bread to nourish us unto life eternal. [*Jn.* 6:55(54)]. O savory Bread, anyone who eats You worthily shall live forever and can never die the eternal death. [*Jn.* 6:50, 52(51), 55, 59]. What an incomparably delightful taste this Bread has for souls who eat It worthily! How wonderful to be nourished on the Bread come down from Heaven, the Bread of angels! [*Ps.* 77(78):23-25; *Wis.* 16:20; *Jn.* 6:33, 41, 50-51, 59(58)]. It is even more wonderful by the love with which It is given to us by Him who is at once both Gift and Giver.

But lest I stay too long on these first two points which feed our understanding, I shall now pass on to the third to inflame our will. It contains something of great spiritual benefit for us. I remark in passing that of all the people then in great numbers in Bethlehem it was only the simple shepherds who came to visit Our Lord. Afterward the Magi came from afar to adore and render homage to our new King lying in the manger.

When they announced the news of this happy birth, the angels gave wonderful signs to the shepherds. Go, they said, and you will find the Infant wrapped in swaddling clothes and lying in a manger. [*Lk.* 2:8-12]. O God, what signs are these to make known Our Lord, and what simplicity the shepherds showed in believing what was announced to them in these words. They would have had some good reason for their belief if the angels had said: "Go, and you will find the Infant seated on an ivory throne, surrounded by heavenly courtiers." But they said: "Your Saviour is born under these signs: you will find Him in a manger among animals, and wrapped in swaddling clothes."

Why do you think the angels addressed the shepherds rather than anyone else in Bethlehem? Our Lord had come as a shepherd and as King of Shepherds. [*1 Ptr.* 5:4]. He desired to favor those like Himself. Whom do the shepherds symbolize? Some say that they represent the shepherds of the Church, such as bishops, superiors of religious, priests and all those who are charged with souls. Some of the holy Fathers insist that Our Lord reveals His mysteries more particularly to them inasmuch as they are commissioned by God to celebrate them and make them understood by their flock, the souls committed to their care.

Others say that the shepherds represent religious and all those who make profession of tending to perfection. But if each one of us is a shepherd and pastor, who are our flock, our sheep? They are our passions, inclinations, affections and spiritual faculties. Note that only the shepherds who were keeping night watch over their flock [*Lk.* 2:8] had the honor and the grace of hearing this gracious news of Our Lord's birth. This is meant to show us that if we do not keep watch over the flock that God has put in our charge, that is, our passions, inclinations and spiritual faculties, feeding them in some holy pastureland, keeping them in order and at their duty, then we will not merit to hear this very lovable news of the Saviour's birth, nor will we be capable of going to visit Him in the manger where His most blessed Mother will place Him tomorrow.

Oh, but the most holy Nativity of Our Lord is a truly great mystery. Each and every one can find in it much consolation, but especially those who are better prepared and have, in imitation of the shepherds, watched carefully over their flocks. At one time we were all unworthy of knowing how to watch over our flocks. As a good shepherd [*Jn.* 10:11, 14] and very lovable pastor of our souls, His sheep for whom He has done so much, Our Lord came Himself to teach us what we ought to do. How happy we will be if we imitate Him faithfully and follow His example. But what does this very sweet Infant do? Look at Him in the manger: "You will find Him," said the angels, "wrapped in swaddling clothes." He certainly does not need to be bound thus. Infants are wrapped in swaddling clothes because, being still tender, if they were not thus bound they might make a false turn and so become maimed. They are also bound so as to prevent injury to their eyes or face. Were their hands free they might strike and harm themselves. After all, they do not yet know any better. Why fear that this might happen to Our Lord, since He had the use of reason from the moment of His Conception? He could not make a false turn, being Uprightness itself.⁵ O God! what goodness in this lovable Saviour! He submitted to doing as other children in order that He might appear as any other poor little baby subject to the necessities and laws of infancy. He truly weeps, but it is not from tenderness over Himself, nor from bitterness of heart, but quite simply to conform Himself to other children.⁶ [*Wis.* 7:3].

There was still another reason why Our Lord wanted to be bound and wrapped and subject to His most holy Mother, letting Himself be handled, carried and wrapped just as it pleased her without showing any annoyance whatever. He wanted to teach us how to govern and rule over our spiritual flock, that is, our passions, affections and spiritual faculties.

There are two principal faculties on which all the others depend, namely concupiscence and irascibility. All other powers, faculties and passions seem to be subject to these two faculties and act only through their commands. By concupiscence we love and desire what seems good and profitable to us. By it we rejoice in prosperity and are saddened in adversity, in mortification, and in all things repugnant to our self-will. Irascibility produces sadness, repugnances, anger, despair and so on. Our Lord wants us to learn from Him how to order these things according to reason. We see Him wrapped and fastened in bands and clothes by His most blessed Mother. He intends thereby to motivate us to bind and fasten with the swaddling clothes of obedience all our passions, affections, inclinations; all our powers, both interior and exterior; our senses, humors and all that we are. Lest we mismanage ourselves He wants us to give up such self-management except insofar as obedience permits it.⁷

See this sweetest of infants who lets Himself be so governed and led by His most blessed Mother that truly it seems that He cannot do otherwise. His sole purpose in this, my dear souls, is to show us what we ought to do, especially religious who have vowed their obedience. Our Lord could never misuse

His will or His liberty. Yet He desired that all should be hidden under these swaddling clothes: His eternal knowledge and wisdom [*Col.* 2:3], all that He was as God, equal to His Father, as well as the use of reason, the power of speaking—in short, all that He was to be when He had attained the age of thirty years. Everything without reserve was enclosed and hidden under the veil of the holy obedience that He bore His Father, who obliged Him to be like all other infants in everything. As St. Paul says, He had to become like His brothers in every way. [*Heb.* 2:17].

What else have we to say except that the mystery of Our Lord's Nativity is also the mystery of the Visitation. Just as the most holy Virgin was to visit her cousin St. Elizabeth, we too must go very often during this octave to visit the Divine Babe lying in the manger. There we shall learn from the sovereign Pastor of shepherds to direct, to govern and to put our flocks in order in such a way that they will be pleasing to His Goodness. But as the shepherds doubtless did not go to see Him without bringing Him some little lambs, we must not go there emptyhanded, either. We must bring Him something. What can we bring to this Divine Shepherd more pleasing than the little lamb which is our love and which is the principal part of our spiritual flock, for love is the first passion of the soul. Oh, how very grateful He will be to us for this present, my dear Sisters, and with what great consolation will the most holy Virgin receive it, through her great desire for our good. This Divine Infant will doubtless look upon us with His benign and gracious eyes as reward for our gift and a sign of His pleasure in receiving it.

Oh, how happy we will be if we visit this dear Saviour of our souls. We will receive from Him an unparalleled consolation. Just as the manna had the taste which each one desired, each one of us will find a special consolation in visiting this most lovable Baby.

The shepherds visited Him and were blessed by Him with very great joy. Returning, they sang God's praises and announced what they had seen to all they met. [*Lk.* 2:20]. But

St. Joseph and the most glorious Virgin received indescribably greater consolations because they assisted Him and remained in His presence, serving Him according to their ability. Both those who went away and those who remained were consoled, but not equally. For each received according to his capacity.

Anna, mother of Samuel, was childless for a very long time. This caused her to be restless and inconstant in her moods. [*1 Kgs.(1 Sam.*) 1:18]. When she saw women rejoicing with their children, she lamented and grew sad because she had none; and when she heard others complain of their children, she rejoiced that God had not given her any. But from the moment she had little Samuel she was never in a bad mood. Doubtless we have had some excuse for our moments of sadness and moodiness while we were without this lovable Infant who was just born for us, or will be born tomorrow. But henceforth it will no longer be right for us to be sad, for in Him we have every reason for joy and happiness.

Bees[8] are restless while they are without a queen. They incessantly flutter hither and yon. There is scarcely any rest in their hive. But as soon as their queen is born, they all gather round her, leaving only for gathering their spoils and, it seems, by her command or permission. In the same way our senses, interior powers and spiritual faculties are like mystical bees. Until they have a ruler, that is, until they have chosen our newly born Lord for their king, they are restless. Our senses ceaselessly wander about, drawing our interior faculties after them, dissipated now on one object they encounter and then on another. There is nothing but a constant waste of time, restlessness and disquietude, all of which shatter the peace and tranquility which are so necessary for our souls. But as soon as they have chosen Our Lord for their king they ought, like chaste and mystical bees, to place themselves near Him, never leaving their hive except for the exercises of charity which He commands them to practice toward their neighbor. Immediately after each charitable exercise they should retire and gather round this most lovable King to distill and store up the honey of the holy and loving thoughts that they draw from the sacred presence of our Sovereign Lord. His simple look into our souls causes unparalleled affections in them, as well as the zeal to serve Him and love Him more and more perfectly.

This is the grace I desire for you, my dear souls: that you remain very near to this sacred Saviour who is about to gather us all around Himself in order to keep us always under the standard of His most holy protection, just like the shepherd who has care of his sheep and of his flock, or like the queen bee who cares so much for her swarm that she never leaves her hive without being surrounded by all her little people. May His goodness grant us the grace to hear His voice, as sheep hear that of their shepherd [*Jn.* 10:27], so that in recognizing Him as our sovereign Shepherd we will not stray away nor listen to the voice of the stranger who remains near us like an infernal wolf, always ready to ruin and to devour us. [*1 Ptr.* 5:8]. May we have the fidelity to keep ourselves submissive, obedient and subject to His wishes and commands, as the bees do with their queen, in order that we might begin in this life what, with the help of God's grace, we shall do eternally in Heaven, where may the Father, Son and Holy Spirit lead us. Amen.

NOTES

1. Cf. p. 51 of this sermon; *Sermons on Our Lady,* "The Visitation," July 2, 1621, p. 156; "The Purification," February 2, 1622, p. 174.
2. It seems that St. Francis de Sales is here distinguishing between the Son's eternal generation as God within the Blessed Trinity and His generation as man on earth. Although as God, the Son is continually and eternally proceeding from the Father, as man He "proceeded" or came forth from the womb of Mary at one particular moment in time.
3. "The nature of the soul" and "that of the body" simply indicate for St. Francis a genuine and integral human nature. He speaks in this manner because he wants three aspects to correspond to the three tastes of the manna for the spiritual reflection he is making at this

point in his sermon.

4. It is doubtful that St. Francis believed literally in this accounting of how bees derive honey from flowers. It is based on readings from Virgil, Aristotle and Pliny. He does find it useful for the spiritual teaching he is giving.

5. In the French this is a play on words.

6. St. Francis teaches here and elsewhere that Our Lord conformed to the exigencies of what it means to be human so as to teach us and give us the preeminent example of truly human behaviour before God and others. Our Lord fully reveals not only who God is, He also fully reveals who we are and how we ought to act.

7. St. Francis is addressing religious, for whom the vow and virtue of obedience are so central.

8. Cf. *Spiritual Conferences*, IX, "Religious Modesty," pp. 144-145.

5

MYSTICAL ASPECTS OF
THE MYSTERY OF CHRISTMAS

Outline for a sermon[1] for the "Vigil of the Nativity of Our Lord, 1614, for the Congregation of the Oblates of the Visitation,"[2] concerning the Saviour as the "Expectation of Nations," Our Lord's two natures: human and divine; the mystery of fruitful virginity, the four kinds of people according to their attitude toward the newborn Divine Infant, the Holy Family as a religious congregation and how they practiced chastity, obedience and extreme poverty, and the various offices of Jesus, Mary and Joseph within this community.

The Church in today's Mass calls this vigil the Expectation of the Redemption and of the Redeemer. O God, You rejoice us each year by the expectation of our Redemption! Jacob had already predicted that the Saviour would be "the Expectation of Nations." [*Gen.* 49:10, Douay; cf. *Agg.* 2:8, Douay]. The Church, too, awaits in expectation: "O Emmanuel, our King and Lawgiver, expectation of the nations and object of their desire, come and save us, O Lord our God." In blessing Joseph, Jacob said: The blessings of your father have been strengthened by those of his ancestors until He comes who is the desire of the eternal hills [*Gen.* 49:26], that is, the Christ. What are these "eternal hills"? Some Fathers take them to indicate the Patriarchs or some especially eminent saints. In my opinion, they indicate the angels.

Since He was to be the Salvation of all, He was certainly expected by all, especially on this night. Note the wonderful expectation of our blessed Lady—"Who will give you to me for my brother, nursed at my mother's breasts that I may find you without, and kiss you, and now no man may despise me." [*Cant.* 8:1].

Therefore, prepare your hearts for the Lord. [*1 Kgs.*(*1 Sam.*) 7:3].

1. Prepare your intelligence by faith in a double mystery. The first mystery is that of the Incarnation. Christ has two natures: divine and human; the divine is incarnate; the human is assumed, without either one eclipsing or destroying the other. Illustrate this point by the bush, burning and yet green. [*Ex.* 3:2]. Also illustrate it by this quotation: "He shall eat butter and honey." [*Is.* 7:15]. Butter is from the earth and is the fat of it; honey is from heaven, of which it is the chrism. The Incarnation is represented in the Old Testament by a number of angels who appeared under human form; it is like the custom of princes dressing their pages in their spouse's colors.

The second mystery is that of virginity. We have already given many comparisons on this mystery. Consider it now under the aspect of myrrh. For Mary is also called "Myrrh of the Sea." Now myrrh produces its drops virginally, as it were. This is the first droplet of myrrh: "My beloved is for me a bundle of myrrh." [*Cant.* 1:12(13)]. It forms drops as of sweat without being pressed. It is like the lily which sheds drops of moisture like grains. Bees bring from heaven a germ from the sun's rays, and this represents the Holy Spirit in the bosom of the Virgin. What admirable fecundity which does no harm to virginity, and what admirable virginity which sanctifies fecundity.[3]

2. Prepare your will by pious thoughts and affections. There are four kinds of people: some do not wish to come—these are the heretics and infidels; others who come seeking something else—these are bad Christians; others who come to adore, like the shepherds and Wise Men; others who come to remain, like the Blessed Virgin and St. Joseph. There are still others, like the angels, who though they leave, nevertheless remain. They are like the best of preachers. They adore the

Lord: "And let all His angels adore Him" [*Heb.* 1:6; *Ps.* 96(97):7]—and they leave in order to preach to others. Yet they remain while leaving, for in spirit they truly remain.

This grotto of Bethlehem is a congregation of oblates. That is why the Blessed Paula founded a community there. It is an admirable form of the religious life! Let us note several marvels about it.

THE VOW OF CHASTITY. "He feeds among the lilies." [*Cant.* 2:16; 6:2]. "Show me where you feed, where you lie down at midday." [*Cant.* 1:6(7)]. With this chastity there is at the same time a great fruitfulness. "Your body is like a heap of wheat, encircled with lilies." [*Cant.* 7:2(3)]. "After her virgins shall be brought to the king." [*Ps.* 44(45):15].

ADMIRABLE OBEDIENCE. The superior in this religious house is Joseph, who is the least of all after Jesus and Mary. Yet the angel always addresses him. This superior might appear not to be very foresightful, since he came to an unprepared shelter. Nevertheless, no one complained in this Holy Family.

EXTREME POVERTY. No one had what is called "mine" or "thine." If anyone possessed something which he could rightfully call his own, it would doubtlessly have been Mary, who had had the Divine Child, for He was her true Son. Yet she did not keep Him entirely for herself, for she said: "Your father and I have been searching for you in sorrow." [*Lk.* 2:48].

In this family are found the three kinds of persons who make up the religious community: superior, Joseph; professed, Mary; novice, Christ. Infirmarian, Mary, whose milk was a healthful tonic for the feeble little Infant. There was no portress because they were in open air. The Babe entoned the sad but pleasing anthems of choir. Mary exercised a number of offices: infirmarian, wardrobian, etc.

But let us consider how well this novice renounces Himself. He is like the queen bee, born with wings. Yet He observes silence with marvelous simplicity. He knew how to speak, and yet He acted like a true infant, etc.

NOTES

1. All that is extant of this sermon is its outline, somewhat enfleshed. (This outline was written in Latin, unlike the sermons.) Yet enough is here to give a fairly clear idea of the directions St. Francis took in addressing his Visitandine nuns that Christmas Eve of 1614.
2. "Oblates of the Visitation" is how the Order of the Visitation was known in its earliest years.
3. It is interesting to speculate on just what nuance St. Francis would develop with each of these examples, but it is clear that he is presenting one basic theme: images of fruitful virginity from nature.

6

THE UNION OF THE DIVINE
AND HUMAN NATURES IN OUR LORD

*Sermon for Christmas Eve, December 24, 1620,
concerning the Incarnation as the work of all three
Persons of the most Holy Trinity, the union of the
divine and human natures in Our Lord, the three
"substances" in Our Lord—Divinity, body and
soul—symbolized by the three tastes of manna:
honey, oil and bread; how man was made God
and God was made man in the Incarnation, man
as a union of body and soul, images of the union
of the humanity and Divinity of Our Lord: iron
inflamed with fire, the fleece of Gedeon, a sponge
in a vast sea; the reason for the Incarnation: to
teach us to live according to reason, as Our Lord
practiced material and spiritual sobriety by depriving Himself of all agreeable things, doing God's
will in all things—and how God does the will of
those who do His; Our Lord's choice of a life of
pains and labors although He could have redeemed
us by a single loving sigh; desire for spiritual consolation vs. humility and resignation to God's will,
and the hidden profundities of the Mystery of the
Incarnation.*

Today we are celebrating the feast of the Expectation of
the glorious Virgin, that is, the coming and birth of our dear
Saviour and Master. I intend to give you a little catechism
on the subject of the Incarnation, not a sermon or an exhor-
tation. According to St. Thomas, everyone ought to know
something of the content of the mysteries of the Faith. They
certainly need not know them as apologetical theologians do.

No, but they ought to know them in a way which is appropriate for the simple faith of Christians. Many try to preach about them and make them understood, but there are too few who have the proper understanding of them. This is why there are many errors held about them. How can we meditate on what we do not really understand? For this reason, catechism is taught to the novices in religious communities. This is done so that they might know their faith and have some understanding of the truths on which they meditate. I will not speak learnedly of the mystery of the Incarnation, but quite simply, so as to be more easily understood. I will divide my talk into three points. We shall consider first who brought about the Incarnation. Secondly, we shall consider what the Incarnation actually is. And finally, we shall see why the Incarnation occurred.

First, we know that the Father gave us His Son, for we read that God so loved the world that He gave His only Son. [*Jn.* 3:16]. Nevertheless, it is not only the Father who brought about the Incarnation, but the Son and the Holy Spirit as well. And although the Incarnation is the work of all three Persons of the Blessed Trinity, only the second Person became incarnate. All the ancient Doctors, but especially St. Bonaventure, used comparisons to help us understand all this. So that it might be clear to you, I will adapt it to the ceremony of clothing. Here is a daughter to whom the habit is being given. The superior and the directress or mistress dress her, placing the habit on her, but she too cooperates in this. Three persons participate in this action, the daughter, the superior and the directress. Nevertheless, there is only one person who is clothed—namely, she who is receiving the habit. It is the same in the Incarnation: the Father and the Holy Spirit bring about the Incarnation, as well as the Son, who Himself becomes incarnate. But neither the Father nor the Holy Spirit becomes incarnate. Only the Son is clothed with the habit of our humanity.

There are many other similar examples for helping us understand this mystery. Take, for instance, the example of a prince who is being clothed in his royal purple: there are two lords vesting him, and the prince who is being vested. Though the other two have the task of dressing him, he also cooperates by moving his arms and hands. Yet of these three persons, only the prince is being clothed. These examples help to make clear that the Incarnation, though the work of all three Persons of the Blessed Trinity, results in the Son alone being clothed with our nature.

Whenever God acts outside Himself, it is the action of all three Persons, Father, Son and Spirit, acting as one principle of operation. Although they are three Persons, yet they are one single God, having only one same wisdom, power and goodness. Though we may attribute power to the Father, and wisdom to the Son, and goodness to the Holy Spirit, yet all Three are omnipotent, all-wise, omniscient and all-good. Thus there is only one God in three Persons, and this God is all-powerful, all-wise and all-good. Yet we name the Father "Lord" and "Creator of Heaven and of earth." But that does not mean that the Son and the Holy Spirit do not share in the creative act as well, since all Three have one same power by which They created all things. Therefore, it is neither the Father alone nor the Holy Spirit alone who wrought the Incarnation, but the Father, the Son and the Holy Spirit, while the Son alone becomes incarnate. So when you are asked who brought about this great mystery, you must answer that it was the work of the most Holy Trinity, but that only the second Person has taken our humanity.

The second point for consideration is: What is the Incarnation? It is what we call the hypostatic union, the union of the human nature with the divine, a union so close that although there are two natures in this little newborn Infant, yet they constitute but one Person. There are three substances in Him, the body, the divine nature, and the soul. This will be made clearer by analogies.

Manna is a figure of the Incarnation of the Word. It also prefigured the Eucharist, as our ancient Fathers have said. However, between the mystery of the Eucharist and that of the Incarnation there is only one difference: in the Incarnation we see the incarnate God in His own Person, and in the Eucharist we see Him under a more hidden and obscure form. In both instances it is the same God-man who was born of the Virgin. Thus, the manna which prefigured the Eucharist can also symbolize the Incarnation. Manna was a kind of food with which the Lord fed the children of Israel. It fell at night and looked like little sugar-coated pills. [*Ex.* 16:13-14; *Num.* 11:7-9]. Some of the Doctors have said it was made in the air by angels. Whether this is so or, as others hold, God Himself made it without the aid of any creature [*Ps.* 77(78):25; cf. *Wis.* 16:20], both opinions can be used to illuminate the mystery of the Incarnation. For God used the angel Gabriel to announce this mystery to Our Lady. [*Lk.* 1:26-28]. On the other hand, no angels brought about this admirable work, but the most Holy Trinity alone, without any creaturely concurrence.

Manna had three distinct tastes: that of honey, that of oil, and that of bread. [*Ex.* 16:31; *Num.* 11:8; *Wis.* 16:20]. These three substances are found in the true Manna, Our Lord [Cf. *Jn.* 6:31-32]: honey represents His divinity, oil His soul, and bread His body. Honey comes not from earth but from heaven.[1] It falls onto beautiful flowers, where it is wondrously preserved until bees come to gather it with unparalleled skill, nourishing themselves upon it. Now, Divinity is that honey which fell from Heaven to the earth into that beautiful flower—the humanity of our Saviour, with which It was joined and united.

Oil comes from neither Heaven nor earth. It does not come from the earth like other plants. Still less does it fall from heaven, as does honey. For olives grow on tall trees. Oil is a liquid which floats on top of all others. As such it represents the second substance in Our Lord, His most holy soul. The human soul does not come from the earth, in that it is not made by our parents. Our lowly bodies are indeed formed from their substance, but the infused soul is not made by them. It being entirely spiritual, God alone is its Creator. Our Saviour's sacred body was formed from the most pure blood of the Virgin, but His most blessed soul was directly created by the Father and the Holy Spirit at the very moment when They formed His body. At the moment the glorious Virgin gave her consent, the Holy Spirit formed the Saviour's body, and at the same time, His most holy soul came to animate it. Our Lord's soul, then, did not come from Heaven or earth, for it did not exist before the Incarnation, but simultaneous with it. It was created at the moment of the Virgin's *fiat.*

The third taste of the manna was that of bread. Now bread clearly comes from the earth. Wheat, from which bread is made, grows from the earth. Bread, then, represents for us Our Lord's third substance. For His most holy flesh was formed from the blood of Our Lady[2] and, in this way, comes from the earth.

Manna had three tastes, but there was only one manna. Similarly, although in Our Lord incarnate there are three substances, there is nevertheless only one Person. For the substance of the soul and that of the body are constitutive of genuine humanity, and this human nature joined together with the divine nature constitutes not two, but one Person, who is both God and man. What a wonderful work of God's providence! Knowing that Divinity was unknown to the human family, the Divine Majesty desired to become incarnate, uniting with human nature so that under this human mantle Divinity could again be acknowledged. I know that from time immemorial Divinity has been known, for all the ancient philosophers have avowed It. But this knowledge was so obscure that it was really unworthy of being called knowledge. Moreover, even when they knew God, they often did not acknowledge Him [*Acts* 17:23; *Rom.* 1:21; *Eph.* 4:17-18], which is far more important. Had Our Lord not become incarnate, He would have remained always hidden in the bosom of His Eternal Father and unknown to us.

Certainly, in the Incarnation He has made us see that which otherwise the human mind could hardly have imagined or understood, that is, that God was man and man God: the immortal, mortal; the one incapable of suffering, suffering—subject to heat, cold, hunger and thirst; the infinite, finite; the eternal, temporal—in short, man divinized and God humanized in such a way that God, without ceasing to be God, is man; and man, without ceasing to be man, is God.[3]

Thus we can say that the Magi who kissed the feet of this newborn little Infant kissed the feet of God. But how can this be so? Since God as God has no body, how can the Magi be said to have kissed His feet? Yet it is so because of the Personal union of the two natures.[4] These two natures are so united that, without being blasphemous, we can say: This blood is the Blood of God, the Blood of a Lamb [*1 Ptr.* 1:19; *Apoc.(Rev.)* 5:12] who died for the sins of humankind. God has been scourged and whipped; the hands of God have been stretched out and nailed to the Cross. This does not mean that God [as God] suffered all this, nor that He shed His Blood or extended His arms on the Cross, for God as God is unable to suffer. He has not endured these things as God, since the Divinity did not suffer in the Passion. The Divinity did not stretch out His hands on the Cross, or shed His blood, for in God there is neither blood, nor arms, nor hands. But we can truthfully speak thus because of the strict union of the human nature with the Divine.

Man is a rational creature composed of soul and body. I am truly a rational creature. To deny it would be a lie. Bodily I am an animal, but because of my spiritual soul I am a rational animal. If you regard a person with a pain in his leg from the perspective of his soul only, you will immediately ask: "How can this spiritual creature say he has a pain? For the soul has no legs, and yet it is the soul which makes us human. How can he say that he extends his arm or has a pain in his arm, since he has neither arms nor legs, the soul being entirely spiritual?" On the other hand, when you see a man talking and regard him from his corporal aspect only and not his spiritual aspect as well, you will be astonished inasmuch as it is a quality of only a spiritual nature to be able to talk and to understand. Now if this man who complains of the pain in his arm or who discourses were composed only of body or only of soul, he could neither discourse nor complain. But because of this strict union between his bodily and spiritual natures, forming but one indivisible person, we can truthfully say that this man, or rational animal, has a pain in his leg or that he is talking or discoursing, understanding these two natures as if they were one. Similarly, because of the strict union between the divine and human natures in Our Lord, we speak of them as if they were one: "Why should I not suffer such a thing, since God has suffered it?"

Analogies will help you to understand this better, not with the same kind of clarity you might have in seeing some sensible object or the understanding you would have of some work like, say, embroidery, but you will have sufficient understanding to believe it correctly. Take an iron plate and cast it into a burning furnace. Then with tongs, withdraw it from the fire. You will see that this plate, which shortly before was only iron, is now so inflamed that you cannot tell whether it is made of iron or fire; for the iron is so inflamed that it appears to be fire rather than iron, so completely have these two natures mingled together. In this condition, you could truthfully say that this fire is a fire of iron, and that this iron is iron that has caught fire. Yet this union is without prejudice to either, for the iron, cast into the fire, does not cease being iron—nor does the fire in the iron cease being fire. You have only to pour water on the hot iron plate, and it will return to its original form.

It is similar with the Divinity and the humanity in Our Lord. The Divinity is, as it were, the burning furnace into which the humanity has been cast, with this humanity so joined to Divinity that it shares now in the divine nature in such a way that man has become God and God has become man, without, in this intermingling, the divine nature and the human nature ceasing to be what they were before. Now, as the iron drawn from the furnace is no longer called simply iron but flaming iron, and the fire, a fire of iron, so we say that in the Incarnation God is humanized and man divinized. But there is an important difference: throwing water on the inflamed iron cools it and it returns to its original form. This does not happen in the union of Divinity and humanity. For from the moment that the divine nature was joined to the human nature, it was never separated from it by any water of tribulation that was cast upon them. They have always remained most intimately united, with an indissoluble and inseparable union. This, then, is the way the mystery of the Incarnation is to be understood.

When Moses wanted to free the Israelites from Egypt, God instructed him on how to go about it. But I have spoken about this before. I will take another story which also suits my purpose. Gedeon was a captain in the army of Israel and desired to know, before engaging in battle with the Madianites, if he would be favored by God. Therefore he asked for a sign. The human spirit is truly amazing![5] He said to the Lord: "I will take fleece (that is, the shearing from a ram or ewe) and stretch it out on that part of the earth used as a threshing floor. If dew falls only on the fleece so that in the morning I find the fleece thoroughly soaked but the earth bone dry, then I will take this as a most certain sign that You will be favorable to me and that we will be victorious over our enemies." He placed the fleece down, and God in His goodness brought about the miracle. Dew fell so heavily from Heaven that the fleece was drenched. But the earth under it remained so dry that it seemed to have been beaten for many days.[6] [*Jgs.* 6:36-40]. Finding the fleece soaking wet with dew, Gedeon took it and wrung it completely dry (a great deal of water was wrung out). Then he successfully engaged in battle.

What does the fleece represent but Our Lord's humanity, upon which the heavenly dew of the Divinity fell with such great abundance that the humanity was divinized. But here too there is an important difference between the analogy and the Incarnation, for we could never find a comparison so round that there would not be something to round off. Gedeon found the fleece completely saturated with dew, with water clinging to its surface, yet not wetting the ground. He wrung out the fleece, releasing the water. But in the Incarnation the two natures, having once become united, are never separated. Divinity, this divine dew, has never left the fleece of humanity, neither in life nor in death. It has always remained in union with Our Lord's body and soul. And even though His body and soul were separated in death, Divinity remained with both the one and the other: with the Saviour's soul in Limbo, and with His sacred body in the tomb. There is also this difference: though it was the fleece that sustained the water, it is not the humanity which sustains the Divinity, but rather the Divinity which sustains the humanity.

Another analogy will make this clearer still. For some reason, poets think it uncivil to speak of the sponge. But certainly since it was presented to Our Lord during His Passion when He said that He was thirsty [*Jn.* 19:28-29], from the moment this sponge touched the sacred lips of the divine Saviour, it has been canonized.[7] Since then it has become an acceptable image for use when speaking of holy things. No longer an incivility to speak of it, it is on the contrary an honorable and becoming thing. For this reason I will use it to help you understand the Incarnation.

Imagine a huge sponge which grew in the sea and had never been used by any creature. In the sea every part of this sponge is filled with water, with the sea above it, beneath it, all around and within it, not the least particle of it that is not saturated with water. But neither the sponge nor the sea loses its nature. Take note of this: although the sea is in all parts of the sponge, the sponge does not absorb the sea, for the great and vast sea cannot be contained in the sponge. This comparison represents very well the union of the human and divine natures.

The sponge symbolizes our Saviour's sacred humanity, and the sea His Divinity. His humanity is so imbued with the Divinity that there is not a single part of Our Lord's body and soul which is not filled with the Divinity, yet without this human nature ceasing to be integrally human. But the humanity is not everywhere that the Divinity is, for the Divinity is like an infinite sea which surrounds and fills everything but cannot Itself be contained by anyone or anything. By these comparisons it is clear what the Incarnation is. When asked what this mystery is, you ought to answer thus: "It is such a union of the human nature with the Divine, such a joining of Divinity with humanity, that by it man became God—and God, taking his nature, became man."

Now to the third point of our reflection: why did the Incarnation occur? It occurred in order to teach us to live no longer like brute animals, as people did after Adam's fall, but with and according to reason. Our Lord came, in fact, to teach us abstinence and sobriety in material things, honors and comforts of this world, to trample all that underfoot while embracing their opposites. Before the Incarnation men lived like brute beasts [*Ps.* 48(49):13, 21], running after this life's honors and pleasures as horses, dogs and other animals go after what they covet. Watch a horse. When it is thirsty and finds a place to quench its thirst, it plunges into the water. Even if it is bridled, there is no way of stopping it. It will drag its rider with it. People who live not according to reason, but according to their disorderly appetites, plunge into the search for sensual satisfactions. Desiring to draw them away from this manner of life, Our Lord became incarnate in order to bridle and check them, teaching them by His works not to value these things at all.

There is no beast, however brutal, who does not recognize the one who is good to him. The horse knows its former stable, because it was given its oats there. The dog knows its master. The same is true of other animals, which seem to have a certain feeling for those who are good to them. [Cf. *Is.* 1:3]. While man was living like a brute animal, Our Lord came to teach him how to live otherwise. He gave him many wonderful examples of sobriety. And there is no one, however deficient in judgment and reason, who, knowing this, would not experience some feeling of gratitude for it.

Now the Saviour also became incarnate to teach us spiritual sobriety, which for Him consisted in a detachment from and a voluntary privation of all the delightful and agreeable things He could have had and received in this life. He willingly and with full consent took upon Himself all the labors and tribulations, poverty and contempt that could be endured in this world. [*Is.* 53:4-5]. His perfectly glorious soul continually enjoyed the clear vision of Divinity, yet He did not wish, for that reason, to be exempt from sorrows. At the moment of His Incarnation He saw and read in the book of predestination all that He was to suffer. This book was entitled *The Holy Will of God.* Now, during His entire life Our Lord did nothing else but read, practice and keep all that He had found written there [*Ps.* 39(40):7-9; *Heb.* 10:5-9], conforming His will to that of His heavenly Father, as He Himself said: "I came not to do My own will, but that of Him who sent Me." [*Jn.* 6:38].

Oh, how happy we would be to read this same book well, and to devote all our efforts to the accomplishment of God's will for us by the renunciation and complete surrender of our own will, with no other concern but to conform our will to His! By this means we would obtain from His goodness all that we could possibly desire. He whose only concern is to do the divine will obtains from His goodness all that he needs. To the extent that one accomplishes this holy will, God does his, as it is written: "The Lord does the will of those who fear Him." [*Ps.* 144(145):19]. You saw how He did all that Gedeon wanted when he asked a sign of Him.

At the moment of His Incarnation our dear Saviour saw all that He was to suffer: the whips and lashes, the nails and thorns, all the injuries and blasphemies that would be spewed out upon Him—in short, all that He must suffer. Extending His sacred arms and offering Himself in unparalleled love to bear all those things, He embraced them and placed them in His Heart with such love that He began from that moment to feel all that He would afterwards suffer during His Passion. From that moment, by a complete detachment,

He deprived Himself of all the consolations that He could have received in this life. The only exceptions were those of which He could not deprive Himself. For our salvation and Redemption, He subjected the lower part of His soul to suffer sadness, pain, fear, apprehension and dread. He did all this not through constraint or because He could not do otherwise, but willingly and with full determination—the better to manifest His love to us.

Certainly, all these sufferings were not necessary for our salvation, for a single act of love, a single loving sigh from His Sacred Heart would have been of infinite price, infinite value, infinite merit.[8] A single one of His sighs would have been enough to redeem not only this world but a thousand worlds, and a thousand thousand human and angelic natures, if there had been that many and had they sinned. Not only a single sigh—a single one of His tears would have been enough to redeem all of them and to satisfy Divine Justice, since it would have been shed from the infinite love of an infinite Person. Our Lord merited more by the breath of a single loving sigh than all the saints, all the cherubim and all the seraphim could ever merit. God was more honored by a single act of love and adoration offered by the most blessed soul of the Saviour at the moment of its creation than He has ever been or ever will be by all the acts of love and adoration of all creatures, both angelic and human. Yet our dear Master did not wish to redeem us by a single sigh. Rather, He willed to suffer a thousand pains and labors, paying in full rigor of justice for our faults and iniquities, teaching us by His example spiritual sobriety, detachment from all consolations, so as to live according to reason and not according to our appetites and affections.

That is why we are in the habit of saying to young girls about to enter this monastery that religion is "a school of abnegation of all wills," a cross on which we must be crucified. In short, we come here to suffer, not be consoled. If you desire sugar and sweets, you had better take yourself to a candy store; for here we eat only bitter food, painful to the flesh but always profitable to the heart. I always say to these girls, and I cannot repeat it too often: "Come now, my dear daughter, what are you really looking for in religion? Consolations?" "Yes." "Then you had better reconsider, for you are deceiving yourself if you expect to be consoled here, to receive and taste spiritual sweets." O God, we must not look for that! Such conduct is insupportable to those who know even the least bit about true devotion. Come here to live in profound humility and complete resignation, ready to accept with equanimity of spirit both desolations and consolations, sweetness and tribulations, dryness and repugnances. If God gives you consolations or sweets, kiss His hand and thank Him very humbly, but do not remain there. Go further, and humble yourself.[9]

Certainly, it is a great pity to see Our Lord suffer so much, deny Himself all the pleasures and consolations He could have received even in the midst of His sufferings, choosing to accept only those of which He could not be deprived, while we, on the other hand, are so in love with these pleasures and consolations that we seem to work only to receive them! However little our consolations may be, we take such great pleasure in reflecting on them and delighting in them that we end up doing nothing worthwhile. These consolations are the delight of certain people who are much too eager for them. They are not really necessary. You are certainly no better for having them. After all, God grants them to both the just and to sinners. Sometimes He even gives many to people in the state of sin, deprived of grace! Why then cling to them so tenaciously?

Consider, I beg you, this little newborn Infant in the manger at Bethlehem. Listen to what He says to you. Look at the example He gives you. He has chosen the most bitter, the poorest things imaginable for His birth. O God! whoever remains close to this manger during the Christmas octave will melt with love in seeing this little Infant in so poor a place, weeping and trembling from the cold. Oh, you will see how reverently the glorious Virgin your Mother kept

looking at His Heart, all aflame with love, as she wiped
the sweet tears which flowed so softly from the gentle eyes
of this blessed Babe! How she ran after the sweet fragrance
of His virtues! [*Cant.* 1:3(4)].

Behold God incarnate! How beautiful it has been to reflect
on the very profound mystery of our Saviour's Incarnation!
But all that we can possibly know and understand from this
reflection is as nothing. We could very well repeat what a
certain wise man said. He had been reading a book by an
ancient philosopher, whose name I cannot recall. It contained
very lofty and obscure thoughts. He frankly admitted: "This
book is so erudite, so difficult, that I scarcely understand
anything of it. The little that I do understand is very beautiful, but I believe that what I do not understand is even more
so." He was right. Using similar words while considering
the mystery of the Incarnation, we could say: "This mystery
is so exalted and so profound that we understand next to nothing about it. All that we do know and understand is very
beautiful indeed, but we believe that what we do not comprehend is even more so. Finally, someday in Heaven above,
we will grasp it fully." There we will celebrate with an incomparable delight this great feast of Christmas, of the Incarnation. There we will see clearly all that took place in
this mystery. We will eternally bless Him who, from His exalted state, lowered Himself in order to exalt us. [Cf. *Phil.*
2:6-7; *Heb.* 2:9]. May God grant us this grace. So be it.
Amen. So be it!

NOTES

1. St. Francis is following the opinion of Virgil, Aristotle and Pliny
   in speaking of honey as a heavenly liquid. His only purpose is to
   make use of it as a fitting image for the Divinity in Jesus.
2. It seems clear that in the early seventeenth century the mother's blood
   was considered constitutive of her child's flesh and blood.
3. Cf. *Sermons on Our Lady,* "The Visitation," July 2, 1621, p. 156;
   "The Purification," Feb. 2, 1622, p. 174; p. 51-52 of this volume.

4. Here St. Francis is using the patristic Christological principle of "exchange of properties" or characteristics. This principle underscores the deep personal (hypostatic) union of the human and divine natures in Jesus by predicating both human and divine properties or characteristics of the one Jesus. Thus, for instance, although God cannot suffer, He can be said to suffer in Jesus, who is both God and man in one Person.

5. It seems that St. Francis is taking umbrage at the audacity of Gedeon in asking for such a sign rather than trusting in God.

6. Used as a threshing floor, the earth can be said to be "beaten."

7. Cf. St. Francis de Sales: *Defense de l'Estendart de la sainte Croix* (*Defense of the Standard of the Cross*), Bk. 1, chap. 4.

8. Cf. *Sermons for Lent*, "The Passion of Our Lord and What It Means," Good Friday, March 25, 1622, p. 183.

9. Cf. *Introduction to the Devout Life*, Part IV, chap. 13.

7

THE INCARNATION

*Sermon for Christmas Midnight Mass, December
25, 1622, concerning the great Christian feasts and
their observance in the early Church, the Incarnation as God's end in creating the world, the
two births of the Word: eternal and temporal, the
two natures of the Word made flesh, and the Eternal Father's goodness to us in making His Son
a member of our human race.*

Among the solemnities of Holy Church there are three which
have been celebrated at all times and which have their original source in that great feast of Passover which was observed
in the Old Law. These three feasts are all called Pasch, or
Passage, or Passover. [*Ex.* 12:11]. Today's feast was instituted
to commemorate Our Lord's passage from His Divinity to
our humanity. The second passage is that from His Passion
and death to His Resurrection, His passage from mortality
to immortality, which we celebrate all during Holy Week and
at Easter. The third passage is celebrated at Pentecost, the
day on which Our Lord adopted the Gentiles [Cf. *Acts* 2:17,
39] and permitted them to pass from infidelity to the happiness of becoming His well-beloved children, the greatest happiness possible for the Church. All these feasts find their
source in today's mystery.

But you may say at this point that it is not usual to preach
at night. And I reply that it was indeed the custom in the
primitive church, while it was in its first flower and vigor.
St. Gregory bears witness to this in his homily for this day.
The early Christians even said the three nocturns of Matins
separately, rising three times during the night for this purpose.

Moreover, they went to choir seven times a day to recite the Office, thereby fulfilling verse 164 of Psalm 118 (119). St. Augustine says that they even preached three times on this feast: first at Midnight Mass, then at the Mass, and finally at the Mass during the day. So great was the fervor of those early Christians that nothing wearied them. The least among them was of greater value than the best of religious of today. We have become so cold since those early days that we must now shorten the Mass, the Office, and sermons. But this is not to the point. Rather, I intend to speak to you first of how we ought to believe the mystery of Christ's Incarnation which the Church sets before us this day, and then of what we should hope for and do in light of this faith. If I do not finish all that I want to say I shall do so later in the day, if God gives us the time.

Before beginning my discourse I wish to remind you that I like to use analogies when I preach. I will do so here too. Now in all that we do or plan, if we are wise we keep its purpose or goal in mind[1] [*Ecclus.(Sir.)* 7:40(36)], for we should have one. For example, if someone intends to build a house or a palace he must first consider whether it is to be a lodging for a vine-dresser or peasant or if it is for a lord, since obviously he would use entirely different plans depending on the rank of the person who is to live there. Now the Eternal Father did just that when He built this world. He intended to create it for the Incarnation of His Son, the Eternal Word.[2] The end or goal of His work was thus its beginning, for Divine Wisdom had foreseen from all eternity that His Word would assume our nature in coming to earth. This was His intent even before Lucifer and the world were created and our first parents sinned. Our true and certain tradition holds that sixteen hundred twenty-two years ago Our Lord came to this world and, in assuming our nature, became man.

Thus we are celebrating the Saviour's birth on earth. But before speaking of that birth let us say something of the Word's divine and eternal birth. The Father eternally begets His Son, who is like Him and co-eternal with Him. He had no

beginning, being in all things equal to His Father. Yet we
speak of the Son being born for us from the Father's bosom,
from His substance, as we speak of the rays coming forth
from the bosom of the sun, even though the sun and its rays
are but one and the same substance. We are forced to speak
thus, recognizing the inadequacy of our words. Were we angels we would be able to speak of God in a far more ade-
quate and excellent way. Alas, we are only a little dust, children
who really do not know what we are talking about. The Son
then, begotten of the Father, proceeds from the Father without occupying any other place. He is born in Heaven of His
Father, without a mother. As sole origin of the Most Blessed
Trinity the Father remains the Virgin of virgins. On earth
the Son is born of His Mother, Our Lady, without a father.
Let us say a word about these two births, for which we have
true and certain proofs, as I said a while ago.

The Evangelist [*Lk.* 1:35] assures us that the Divine Word
became flesh in the most holy Virgin's womb when the angel
announced to her that the Holy Spirit would come upon her
and that the power of the Most High would overshadow her.
This is not, of course, to say that in Jesus Christ there are
two persons. In the hypostatic union, the Word become flesh
is true God and true man, and this without any separation,
from the moment of His Conception. Some examples may
help. Naturalists tell us that honey is made of a certain gum
called "manna," which falls from the sky, and unites or mixes
with flowers which in turn draw their substance from the
earth. In joining together, these two substances result in the
one honey.[3] In our Lord and Master, Divinity has similarly
united our nature with His own, and God has made us sharers
of the Divine nature in some fashion [*2 Ptr.* 1:4], for He
was made man like us. [*Phil.* 2:7; *Heb.* 4:15].

Note that there is a difference between honey collected from
thyme and all other kinds. It is much more excellent than
that called heraclean, which is made from the aconite and
other flowers. As soon as we taste it we recognize that it
is from thyme, because it is both bitter and sweet. Heraclean

honey, on the other hand, causes death.[4] It is similar with Our Lord's sacred humanity. Springing from Mary's virginal soil, His humanity is very different from ours, which is wholly tainted by corruption and sin. Indeed, because the Eternal Father willed His only-begotten Son to be the Head and absolute Lord of all creatures [*Col.* 1:15-18], He willed that the most holy Virgin should be the most excellent of all creatures, since He had chosen her from all eternity to be the Mother of His Divine Son.[5] In truth, Mary's sacred womb was a mystical hive in which the Holy Spirit formed this honeycomb with her most pure blood. Further, the Word created Mary and was born of her, just as the bee makes honey and honey the bee, for one never sees a bee without honey nor honey without a bee.

At His birth we have very clear proofs of Our Lord's Divinity. Angels descend from Heaven and announce to the shepherds that a Saviour is born [*Lk.* 2:8-14] to them. Magi come to adore Him. [*Matt.* 2:1-11]. This clearly shows us that He was more than man, just as, on the contrary, His moaning as He lies in His manger shivering from the cold shows us that He was truly man.

Let us consider the Eternal Father's goodness. Had He so desired He could have created His Son's humanity as He did that of our first parents, or even given Him an angelic nature, for it was in His power to do so. Had He willed to do so Our Lord would not have been of our nature. We would not then have had any alliance with Him. But His goodness was such that He made Himself our brother in order that He might both give us an example [*Rom.* 8:29; *Heb.* 2:11-17] and render us sharers in His glory. It was for this reason that He willed to be of Abraham's seed, for the most holy Virgin was indeed of Abraham's race, for it is said of her: Abraham and his seed. [*Lk.* 1:55; *Rom.* 1:3; *Gal.* 3:16].

I leave you at the feet of this blessed Mother and Child so that, like little bees, you may gather the milk and honey that flow from these holy mysteries and her chaste breasts, while waiting for me to continue, if God grants us the grace and gives us the time.[6] I beg Him to bless us with His benediction. Amen.

NOTES

1. Cf. *Sermons for Lent,* "Eternal Happiness," February 20, 1622, p. 61.
2. Cf. *Treatise on the Love of God,* Book II, chap. 4, 5.
3. Cf. *Sermons on Our Lady,* "The Purification," February 2, 1622, p. 174.
4. Cf. *Introduction to the Devout Life,* Part III, chaps. 17, 20.
5. Cf. *Sermons on Our Lady,* "The Immaculate Conception," December 8, 1622, p. 193-195.
6. St. Francis de Sales died just three days later.

8

SPIRITUAL CIRCUMCISION
AND THE SACRED NAME OF JESUS

*Sermon for the Feast of the Circumcision of Our
Lord, January 1, 1622, concerning Christian feast
days, circumcision in the Old Law, Our Lord's
Circumcision, the spiritual circumcision of the part
of ourselves most affected by sin, complete spiritual
circumcision vs. that which is only partial or a
mere incision, observance of the entire Law of God
as necessary for salvation, the greater obligation
of priests, bishops and religious to practice complete spiritual circumcision, the never-ending struggle in this life against unruly passions and
emotions, our inculpability in feeling spontaneous
unruly emotions vs. culpability in those voluntarily encouraged or expressed in words, how it is
far better to be "circumcised" by another than
by oneself, the rape of Dina and the willing sub-
mission to circumcision by the people of Sichem,
the fittingness of Our Lord's reception of the name
of Jesus ("Saviour") on the day of His Circumcision, His three essential titles, Jephte and the password "Scibboleth," and the sacred name "Jesus"
as our password for entering Heaven.*

> *"When the eighth day arrived, on which the
> Child was to be circumcised, he received the
> name of Jesus." —Lk.* 2:21

The days, months, and years all belong to God, who made
and created them. The ancients had so arranged these days
and years that they named and identified them according to

the phases of the moon and named them after their false gods, such as Mercury, Mars, Jupiter and the like. So widespread was this superstition that it was very difficult to uproot. To eradicate it, the Church dedicated feast days to the saints and has preferred for ordinary days, the word "ferial" in place of the names used by the ancient pagans. But even though some of our feasts are dedicated to the saints, *all* are consecrated to Our Lord, who made them and to whom they all belong. This is why the Church dedicates to Him this feast which occurs on the first day of the year, and through it the entire year is dedicated to Him.

Today we are celebrating the Feast of the Circumcision of our divine Saviour when, after His Circumcision, He received the sacred name of Jesus. The story of the Circumcision is wonderfully beautiful, and it is a figure of the spiritual circumcision[1] we all ought to undergo. Although the shortest of all those read during the year, today's Gospel [*Lk.* 2:21] is nevertheless lofty and very profound, for it mentions blood and the name of Jesus, and in these two words the whole story of the Circumcision is told.

I will follow the structure of the Gospel and divide this sermon into two points. In the first, we will talk about the nature of circumcision and our own spiritual circumcision; in the second, we will discuss how reverently the sacred name of Jesus is to be pronounced.

Concerning the first point, circumcision was a kind of sacrament in the Old Law [*Gen.* 17:10-14; *Lev.* 12:3] and signified purification from the stain of Original Sin. It was like a profession of faith in the expectation of Our Lord's coming. Those circumcised became children and friends of God instead of His enemies, as they had been before.

Of course, our divine Saviour had no need of circumcision. Not only was He the Law's Maker, but He had no stain or trace of sin whatsoever. He was the unspotted [*1 Ptr.* 1:19] and all-holy Son of God. From the moment of His Incarnation, He was filled with every kind of grace and blessing of body and soul. Because of that strict union of the humanity with the Divinity, He not only overflowed with the fullness of grace, but His all-glorious soul enjoyed the clear vision of God continually. Thus there was no need whatsoever to subject Himself to the Law of Circumcision. Nevertheless, He willed to submit Himself to it. Also, circumcision distinguished the people of God from other peoples. But Our Lord had no need of being marked with this sign of distinction since He Himself was the seal or very stamp of the eternal Father. [*Heb.* 1:3]. Innumerable are the interpretations and reasons demonstrating why the Saviour was in no way subject to this law, but it would require a great deal of time to present them all. Let it suffice to say, then, that He was in no way obliged to submit to it and that He willingly submitted to it only in order to give us an outstanding example of the spiritual circumcision which we ought to undergo.

Circumcision is performed on the part of the body most damaged by Adam's sin. This is the first remark made by the early Fathers and, if I am not mistaken, by St. John Chrysostom. Their point is to show us that our spiritual circumcision ought to be done on that part of our person most damaged. Many, if not all, Christians are willing enough to undergo spiritual circumcision in order to take part in today's feast, but unfortunately they make this circumcision in that area which needs it the least! There are some who are imprisoned in sensual pleasures (I will use this example, although it is a little gross, until I can recall another). They are in constant pursuit of these brute pleasures. When they want to undergo a spiritual circumcision they take money and give alms. Now of course it is a good thing to circumcise one's wallet in this way and give alms. The Apostle assures us that almsgiving is a good thing. [Cf. *1 Tim.* 6:18; *Heb.* 13:16]. It is always a good practice. But do you not see that that spiritual circumcision is not what is really needed in this case? Do not circumcise your wallet, you pleasure-seeking people, for your sickness is not there. Rather, circumcise your heart, by cutting off evil language, friendships and conversations;

cut off this evil flirting and other such foolishness. Begin
there if you want to undergo a good circumcision. But they
do not do it. Instead, they continue to follow their animal
instincts while congratulating themselves on giving alms, fully
convinced that they have satisfied everything in that.

There are others greedy to amass and possess all sorts of
riches, goods and comforts. Wanting to circumcise themselves,
they keep vigils and observe great fasts and abstinences. They
wear a hair shirt, belts, and all the rest. And in doing all
this, they consider themselves almost saints! O God! what
nonsense! Vigils and fasts are good, but you are not on target
in this spiritual circumcision because you have not begun
where it is most needed. The evil is in your heart, and you
kill your body. You must circumcise your purse, distributing
your goods to the poor. Uproot from your heart that unre-
strained greed for riches, honors, and conveniences which
is found there. Skillfully and ruthlessly apply the knife of
circumcision to your heart and to those affections most
damaged by sin.

Other people perform great penances and austerities, afflict-
ing their bodies with all kinds of pains and hardships. These
same people have no difficulty in drinking in the blood of
their neighbor by a tongue which slanders and detracts.[2] Oh,
poor people, you think you are well circumcised by wearing
the hair shirt, taking the discipline, and doing other such
things; but do you not see that the part you must circumcise
is your tongue, which laps up the blood of the innocent?
[*Ps.* 63(64):4].

There are yet others who circumcise their tongues remarka-
bly and are resolved to keep a deeply profound silence. But
they continually go around growling and grumbling in their
heart, and are full of murmurings and antipathies. Ah, my
dear souls, what are you doing? The evil is hidden in your
heart; so it is not enough to circumcise your tongue. You must
circumcise that part in which are born these grumblings, murmurings and inner angers, because the circumcision ought to
be performed in the place most affected by the sickness of sin.

This, then, is what spiritual circumcision means: to search into one's passions, affections, humors and inclinations in order to root out and cut off any excess in them. To do this a careful and serious examination of conscience is needed in order to recognize what is the most stricken part and what is our inordinate passion, inclination or humor, so that this interior circumcision can begin there.

The second point I wish to emphasize is that this was a circumcision and not an incision. There is a great difference between the two. An incision is required to remove any infection in a sick person's wound or sore. But this is not the same as circumcision, and most Christians make incisions instead of circumcisions. They may make some effort to deal with an infected member, but they do not use the knife to cut and root out from their heart what is superfluous. Now this must be said by way of preface: all are obliged to perform this circumcision, but in different ways, not equally. Priests, bishops and religious have a particular obligation to do it and in a manner completely different from those who live in the world, since they are more especially dedicated to Our Lord.

There are some Christians who cut off everything that keeps them from observing the Law of God. They are very happy indeed, and will reach Paradise in the end. For to attain it we have only to observe the divine commandments.[3] [*Matt.* 19:17]. There are others who are content to correct and to uproot one passion or sinful habit, but who continue to wallow and revel in thousands of other sins against the Lord's Law. These do not perform a circumcision, but only an incision. They fail to penetrate to the corrupted part and to cut out what is needed for a true circumcision. Instead, they are content to strike at one affected member, and that is usually not the sickest. Still, they believe that they have performed a complete circumcision.

And so you will find people in the world who wallow in the vile filth of a thousand sins and who are enchained by many passions and depraved affections. If you question them about what they are doing or have done, they will answer that they have done nothing wrong whatsoever. "Oh!" they say: "We have not killed or stolen; we are not thieves or murderers." That may be true, but that is not enough. There may be other sins which you have committed which are as dangerous as those you have not committed. There are not just two precepts in God's Law; there are many others which one must observe to be saved. To seriously infract one of God's commandments is to judge and condemn oneself to the pains of Hell. When the Lord gave the Law to Moses, He did not say that only those who kill or steal will die; He promised the same threat and punishment with reference to the other commandments as well.

It is undeniably true that only those who have obeyed the Law of the Lord in its entirety will enter Paradise. [*Matt.* 5:19; *Jas.* 2:10]. The entire Law, not just a part of it. The person making only an incision will be condemned, as will be the one who is content to observe one or two commandments, struggling to uproot the evil that keeps one from their observance. To do this and not to be concerned with circumcising the habits of vice which render him rebellious to the other precepts of God will be the cause of his condemnation. It is obvious, then, that everyone must practice spiritual circumcision, though not all equally or in the same manner. But generally speaking, all of us ought to cut and drive the knife not only into one place, as do those who make an incision, but all around it, keeping and observing the Law in its entirety, omitting nothing. In doing this we will be very happy. Thus marked with this spiritual circumcision, we will be recognized as God's children and gathered into His glory at the end.

As for us bishops, priests and religious, dedicated and consecrated to divine service, we are more obliged than others to this spiritual circumcision.[4] We ought to practice it not only as the laity do, but in an even deeper manner, to which they are not obliged inasmuch as they do not enjoy the same means as we; nor are they vowed to Our Lord as we are.

Religious cannot be content with cutting out and combatting a vice or an evil inclination; they must go all around the heart. Making use of a rigorous examination of conscience, they must take special care to scrutinize and note exactly their passions, moods, propensities, aversions and habits to circumcise them.

There are still some religious who make this examination twice daily in order to know well and understand the state of their heart. After this, they make use of the knife of circumcision to scrape away all that is superfluous and dangerous, excising both the sickness and anything which might cause the slightest disturbance or obstacle in the spiritual life. This knife is none other than a good and strong resolution which permits them to ride over all the difficulties involved and to perform this interior circumcision generously. This is why religious life is often called a sanatorium or hospital where not only dangerous and terminal sicknesses are cured, but even minor ones as well. Indeed, one goes much further, purging the least little blemish, the slightest thing which can hinder the spiritual life and, ever so little, delay perfection. Even the sources of evil are removed, as the knife cuts all around the heart. For the heart is the part one must always cut open in this interior circumcision, careful to see and root out its evil thoughts, desires, passions and inclinations; its evil sentiments, repugnances and aversions. Those who do this are truly most happy.

But someone will surely say to me: "All this is true. I have often used the knife to cut out such and such passions and inclinations and such and such repugnances and aversions which I found in my uncircumcised heart waging a cruel war within me. Yet it seems that all that amounts to very little! Despite my great care and diligence, I still experience strong and powerful passions, aversions, disgusts, repugnances and many other movements which struggle and do battle with me." We reply: "Ah, my dear souls, we have come here not to enjoy ourselves, but to suffer. Be patient and one day you will be in Heaven, where there will be only

peace and joy. There you will not feel any passion, or movements of envy, aversion, or repugnance, since you will possess an enduring tranquillity and rest. It is only there that
we enjoy ourselves, not in this life, where one must suffer
and be circumcised." If there existed someone here who had
no passion, that person would not suffer but would be in
absolute bliss. Such cannot be nor ought it to be, for as long
as we live we will have passions. We will never be free of
them until death, because it is precisely in the struggle with
these passions and emotions that our victory and triumph
lies. This is the universal opinion of the Doctors and the
teaching of the Church.

I am well aware that in the past there were hermits and
anchorites in Palestine who claimed that careful and frequent
mortification would enable one to reach a state without passions or movements of anger, a state in which one would
receive an affront without turning red, or be injured, mocked
and beaten without feeling any emotion whatsoever. Their
opinion has been condemned as false and rejected by the
Church, which in response has declared—and it is true—that
as long as we live upon this earth we will have passions,
feel the stirrings of anger, revulsions, attachments, inclinations, repugnances, aversions and all other such things human.

We should not be surprised, then, if when someone tells
us our faults or reprimands us we promptly feel these stirrings, or even suffer them for a long time. Nor should we
be surprised if we dislike things which run counter to our
inclinations—even less if we should like one thing more than
another. Oh, certainly not! For these are natural passions
and in no way sinful in themselves. There is no reason to
think that in feeling these emotions and repugnances you have
sinned and offended even in the slightest degree. Oh, not
at all, for these stirrings are spontaneous and independent
of us! These diverse emotions of the heart are in no way
culpable, and it is not to these that we are to bring to bear
the knife of circumcision.

Some people fool themselves into thinking that perfection

consists in feeling nothing! So when they experience some stirring of the passions, it seems to them that all is lost. Oh, you poor people, do you not see that this is not the part of you that is most ill nor the part that needs circumcision, for these stirrings are beyond your power?

But what then should I circumcise? Circumcise the consequences of these emotions; cut off the words which result from them. Oh, worldly people! Circumcise those blasphemies, swearings, injurious words and detractions which are born of your anger and which are truly sinful and mortally sick. My dear souls, circumcise those murmurings reflected upon, weighed, and nurtured in your hearts for days, weeks and entire months, as well as those voluntarily encouraged repugnances against the things which obedience demands and which run counter to your tastes and fancies. Probe your heart, carefully scrutinize your passions, inclinations and affections; then root up and cut out all of this forthrightly and completely. Do not be content just to make incisions like the worldly, but perform good circumcisions which are spiritual and interior. This, then, is the second consideration which I want to make concerning today's Gospel.

The third is this: in the Old Law, those to be circumcised did not circumcise themselves, but were circumcised by the hand of another. Now our Saviour willed to be like us in all things and subject Himself to the Law without any exception; therefore, He willed also to be circumcised not by His own hand but by the hand of another, no matter who it might be. I am well aware that the ancient Fathers and Doctors interpreted this in various ways, but I am not going to repeat them now. I will mention only one of them: Our Lord willed to be circumcised by another for our example, to show us that although it is a good thing to be circumcised by one's own hand, it is even better to be circumcised by someone else's. Surely those ancient solitaries—hermits and anchorites—who lived in the desert are to be admired.[5] We ought to esteem the wonderfully triumphant victories they won by mortifying and circumcising their hearts and interior passions

with the help of God's grace, inspired and prompted by the
Holy Spirit, the saints and their good angels. Yet the circumcision which we endure from others far exceeds theirs, because it is more painful and therefore more meritorious.

All Christians are bound to be spiritually circumcised by
one another. Beyond this there are always people in religious
orders and communities who attentively and continually watch
over their own heart so as to know what ought to be wrenched
out and mortified. For this purpose they keep a knife continually at hand to circumcise themselves. This, however, does
not make them unwilling to be circumcised by others, and
without doubt this latter circumcision is far more acutely painful than the former. We find arrogant, proud, haughty and
coarse people who nevertheless are very cognizant that these
passions are a major hindrance to God's grace and must be
circumcised. They pray with hearts inflamed with this desire. In fact, turning inward, they begin to do it so fervently
that it actually seems painless, and they experience such delight and consolation that they shed abundant tears of deep
spiritual joy. In short, what comes from our own willing and
effort costs almost nothing, so incredibly subtle is our self-love.

But if at this point someone were to tell them: "You are
a lout, a bore," oh, surely their blood would begin to boil
and they would immediately feel the on-rush of anger. This
would be intolerable, and they would find clever words to
justify themselves. Thus, you can see how necessary it is
that someone else guide the knife which circumcises us. Others
know much better than we precisely where the application
is needed.

The preeminent Apostle, St. Peter, was seized with violent
anger when, in the Garden of Olives, he saw the soldiers
coming to take his good Master. He asked Our Lord whether
he should strike with the sword. It is as if he meant: "I
have only a small knife, but if You want I shall strike these
scoundrels, making of them a veritable carnage." Too angry
to wait for the answer, he struck one of the soldiers and
cut off his right ear. But our divine Saviour did not approve

of this action and reprimanded him. He then took Malchus' ear and healed him. Turning to St. Peter, He said: "Put your sword back in its sheath." [*Matt.* 26:51-52; *Lk.* 22:49-51; *Jn.* 18:10-11]. By this He meant: "You have not used your knife to circumcise the part that most needed to be cut out. You have cut off the right ear, which is used to receive spiritual matters such as inspirations and good movements. But you have allowed the left ear, which listens to worldly and vain things, to remain. You ought to have removed the left, not the right ear. For the right ear is ready and eager to hear divine inspirations and heavenly words. By not severing the left ear, the circumcision is not rightly performed." You see, then, how necessary it is to bring the knife to bear on the part that is most sinful and sick.

Time is running out. Therefore I will conclude with a story. Then I will say a word on the second part of today's Gospel. The preacher at the cathedral today began his sermon by relating a remarkable incident which I will now share with you. It is certainly a dish worthy for serving at two tables. With it I will conclude my sermon.

It is recorded in the book of Genesis [*Gen.* 33:18-20; 34] that one day Jacob, with his children and very large family, set up tents near Sichem. Jacob had a very beautiful daughter, Dina. Being near the royal city, Dina was eager to visit it. She decided to go alone to take a look at it. How typical of the human spirit! She goes not only to look around, but also, I believe, to be admired, for she was beautiful and knew it. Alone in this great city of Sichem, she kept marvelling at all she saw. The king's son happened to see her from his window. Taken with her rare beauty, he inquired who she was. (This young prince was actually named Sichem, and his father was Hemor.) He was so taken by her that he had her kidnapped. This was easy enough to do because there are always plenty of people willing to help the great with their evil plans. Carried off, she was dishonored by Prince Sichem. A great uproar ensued, especially because King Hemor and Prince Sichem were not of Dina's nationality.

Finding out what had happened, and knowing how dearly his son loved Dina, Hemor was eager to remedy the situation. Scripture tells us that the heart of Sichem was bound to Dina. [*Gen.* 34:3]. But the bond was not that strong. It was an empty and fragile love like all worldly loves, which last all so briefly. God's love is nothing like that. It remains and never departs from the soul it has entered. It continues to unite and bind the soul to the Divine Majesty not for two or three days like worldly love, but for all eternity. Worldly love, on the contrary, is foolish, dangerous and worthy of condemnation. It stems from and is sustained by foolishness, silliness and stupidity. To please his son, Hemor went to Jacob to arrange for his son's marriage with Dina. Since he was king, many people argued for the marriage, and it was almost settled.

The machinations of the human spirit are strange indeed. Simeon and Levi were Dina's brothers, and they knew that their father, Jacob, was negotiating the marriage of their sister to Sichem. They were shocked at the dishonor Sichem had committed in raping Dina and decided to propose a condition to the King without which they would not consent to the marriage. They demanded that if he wanted an alliance with their nation, all his people would have to be circumcised. At first there was considerable objection to this proposal; but in the end, after much negotiation, it was resolved to propose circumcision to the people of the land of Sichem. When they were all assembled at the place appointed for the consultation, circumcision was proposed to them and various arguments were offered to encourage their agreement with the King's plan for his son's happiness. They were told that Jacob was a great nation and that he would join his people with them, which would strengthen both with more troops. In the end, after much discussion, all agreed to submit to circumcision. It was painful indeed, and the majority were half dead from weakness. Knowing this, Simeon and Levi stormed the city, put everything to the torch, and avenged in blood the evil which Hemor's son had done to their sister.

In this story I note particularly the people's promptitude and acquiescence in submitting to the King's will, placing their own lives in danger so as to please the King's son. O God, shall we flee our spiritual circumcision in cowardice and fear, seeing our Saviour submit Himself today to this same law of circumcision in order to give us an example? In pouring out His blood, He invites us not to shed ours, but only to pour out our hearts and spirits before Him. [*1 Kgs.* (*1 Sam.*) 1:15; *Ps.* 61(62):9; *Lam.* 2:19]. We are invited to this interior circumcision not for His profit and pleasure, but for our good, our salvation and our benefit. Will we refuse, after all this, to do what He asks of us? We see the people of Sichem submit to a very painful law solely to please the King's son. Are we to be so timid and cowardly as to refuse to submit to things which, by contrast, are so mild and easy?

But let us conclude with a word on the name which was given to Our Lord today. We will close with another story. Today's Gospel would have us understand that the shedding of Jesus' blood is related to His name. It is appropriate that He be given this name on the day of His circumcision, for He could not be Saviour without pouring out blood, nor give blood without being Saviour. He could, of course, have saved the world without shedding His blood, but that would not have been enough to satisfy the love He bears us.[6] He could certainly have satisfied divine justice for all of our sins by a single sigh from His Sacred Heart, but this would not have satisfied His love, which desired that by taking the name of Saviour He should give His blood as a deposit of that which He willed to pour out for our redemption. The name of Saviour was rightly given Him on this day, for there is no redemption without shedding of blood [*Heb.* 9:22] and no salvation without redemption, since no one can enter Heaven except by this gate. Also, by making Himself Saviour and Redeemer of mankind, Our Lord begins, in taking this name, to pay our debts with no other money than that of His Precious Blood. He was, then, called Jesus, which means Saviour. [*Matt.* 1:21].

All the ancient Fathers agree that, notwithstanding His many names and titles, Our Lord has only three which belong to Him essentially. The first is that of Supreme Being, reserved only to Him and applicable to no other. [*Ex.* 3:14-15; *Is.* 42:8]. In this name He knows Himself through Himself. The second is that of Creator, which also can be given only to Him, since no one else but Him is Creator. In this name He knows Himself through Himself, but He also knows Himself through His creatures. The third name is Jesus, which likewise belongs only to Him alone, since no one else can be Saviour. [Cf. *Acts* 4:12]. Beyond this there is the title of "Christ" [*Matt.* 1:16], which means High Priest, Anointed One of God. We Christians participate in these last two names. [*1 Ptr.* 2:9; *Acts* 4:12]. In this present life we bear the name of Christ, namely "Christians," and we are anointed by the Sacraments which we receive. When we are in Heaven, we will bear the name of the Saviour inasmuch as there we will all enjoy complete salvation and be among those saved. Thus in Heaven we will be called by Our Lord's other name, Jesus or Saviour, since we will be saved.

Now, how are we to pronounce the sacred name of Jesus so that it may be beneficial and profitable to us? This I am going to tell you by a story, with which I will conclude. This name certainly ought not be pronounced carelessly or thoughtlessly. It is not enough to be aware that it is a two-syllable word, nor even less to speak it merely with the mouth. Parrots can do that! Infidels and Mohammedans name Him perfectly well, as far as that goes, but they are not saved thereby. Our Lord showed us how we are to say it. He shed His blood in receiving His name. In that, He indicated His willingness to do what this holy name signifies: to save.

It is not enough to say it with your lips; it must be engraved upon your heart. Oh, how happy we would be to have alive in us all that our titles signify! For instance, it is not enough to call ourselves priest, bishop, or religious. Our actual lives must be congruent with these titles. We must take care of the charge we exercise and of the vocation in which we live. In short, we must assess how well our passions and affections are controlled and how submissive our judgment is, and whether our actions are congruent with our state in life.[7]

It is recounted in the Book of Judges [*Jgs.* 11, 12] that the great captain Jephte was victorious against the Ammonites by a vow which he made to the Lord. After his daughter's tragic death and all his other troubles, Jephte hoped that he would finally have peace and rest. But this was not to be, for a sedition was stirred up. The sons of Ephraim reproached him for not having invited them to war, although they were brave soldiers. They believed he had acted thus to slight them. Astonished to hear of this new trouble, good Jephte said to them: "Oh, my dear friends, you know very well that I invited you, but you excused yourselves; this is why when the moment came for me to attack, I did." Unwilling to listen to his arguments, they declared war on him. God, however, took Jephte's part because it was just, and so favored him that he slaughtered forty-two thousand and routed astonished Ephraim completely. Then Jephte placed a guard and sentinels on the banks of the Jordan with a watchword: "Ask anyone who wants passage who they are. If they answer that they are from Ephraim, kill them; and if they deny it, make them give the password, *'Scibboleth.'* If they say *'Sibboleth,'* put them to death; but if they say *'Scibboleth,'* give them free passage." *"Scibboleth"* and *"Sibboleth"* are almost the same word (*"Scibboleth"* means "ear of corn" and *"Sibboleth"* means "charge"), but *"Scibboleth"* is uttered gutterally and *"Sibboleth"* is said more lightly.[8]

How happy we will be if, at the hour of our death, as well as during the whole of our lives, we pronounce the sacred name of the Saviour with due respect.[9] It will be like a password by which we will freely enter Heaven, for it is the name of our redemption. In our last hour, if God gives us the grace not to die suddenly, we will have a priest near us who will hold a blessed candle in his hands and will call out to us: "Remember our Redeemer; say 'Jesus,' say 'Jesus.' " Blessed will they be who pronounce it reverently and with a most profound appreciation of our Saviour having ransomed us with His blood and by His Passion. Those who call upon the name well at the time of death will be saved. The opposite will be the fate of those who do not speak it well and who pronounce it tepidly and without fervor. We ought most certainly to repeat it often during our lifetime, for it was given to His Son by the Eternal Father. It is a name which is above every other name, wholly divine, gentle and full of goodness. It is an oil poured out [*Cant.* 1:2(3)] to heal all the wounds of our souls. At this sacred name every knee bends. [*Phil.* 2:9-10]. It is the name which gives joy to the angels, saves men, and causes demons to tremble. This is why it should be deeply engraved upon our hearts and our spirits so that, blessing it and honoring it in this life, we may be worthy of singing with the blessed: Live Jesus! Live Jesus!

NOTES

1. This is an example of how mystical writers appreciate the spiritual significance of physical things.
2. Cf. *Introduction to the Devout Life,* Part I, chap. 1.
3. Cf. *Sermons on Our Lady,* "The Presentation of Our Lady," November 21, 1619, pp. 79-80; "The Presentation of Our Lady," November 21, 1620, p. 129.
4. Cf. *Sermons for Lent,* Thursday of Third Week, "Proper Conduct in Illness," March 3, 1622, p. 102.
5. Cf. *Sermons on Our Lady,* "The Purification," February 2, 1622, pp. 184-185.
6. Cf. *Sermons for Lent,* Good Friday, "The Passion of Our Lord and What It Means," March 25, 1622, p. 185.
7. Cf. pp. 10-11 of this volume.
8. Cf. *Controversies,* Part II, chap. 1, art. 2.
9. Cf. *Sermons for Lent,* Thursday after Fourth Sunday, "Proper Fear of Death," March 10, 1622, p. 142.

THE WEDDING FEAST OF CANA

*Sermon for the Second Sunday after the Epiphany,
January 17, 1621, concerning Our Lord's miracle
at the wedding feast of Cana as the first sign He
performed to manifest His glory, mystical correspondences between the works of Our Lord, His changing of water into wine at the beginning of His
ministry and of wine into Blood at its end, the
attendance of Our Lord and His Mother at the
wedding feast of Cana, Our Lady's way of addressing her Son regarding the shortage of wine,
how we should make the proper intentions in our
prayers, the error of praying for the feelings of
the virtues rather than for the virtues themselves,
the true meaning of Our Lord's seemingly harsh
response to His Mother, Our Lady's confidence
that He would grant a favorable response, the way
in which Our Lord advanced His "hour" in response to Our Lady's prayer, the Holy Eucharist,
and how we should follow Our Lady's advice to
do whatever her Son tells us—by faithfully fulfilling the duties of today so that He may change
the tepid water of our repentance into the wine
of divine love.*

There are two Gospels today: one for confessors,[1] the other
which relates Our Lord's first miracle, worked at the wedding feast of Cana in Galilee. [*Jn.* 2:1-11]. I will speak on
the latter; we will not speak on St. Antony, because in the
cathedral sermon today he was suitably and exhaustively ex-
tolled. I will deal with the first miracle or, as St. John calls
it, the first sign that Our Lord performed to manifest His

glory. First we shall discuss how the miracle was accomplished, and secondly, by whom it was accomplished and who took part in it. The Evangelist declares that this was the first sign that Jesus performed to manifest His glory. I am well aware that some doctors argue that this miracle was not Our Lord's first. But since not only St. John attests to it, but even St. Ambrose, and since the vast majority of ancient Fathers agree, we accept it too. In order better to develop the views of St. Ambrose and other Fathers on this miracle, difficulties with their view need to be dealt with first, after which we will give a reflection which will be a consolation that our faith gives us.

Let us begin by saying that this miracle was the first sign that the Saviour *Himself* gave to manifest His glory. Many prodigies, it is true, were wrought before this one: some by Our Lord, others in Our Lord, and others for the coming of Our Lord—as the Incarnation, the greatest of all and the miracle of miracles. But the Incarnation was invisible, secret and unknown. So exalted is it that it infinitely surpasses the comprehension of the angels and archangels. Consequently it did not serve as a sign to manifest the glory of God as did that performed at the wedding feast of Cana. The Incarnation is so preeminent and profound a mystery that it was never anticipated—nor could it be—by the ancient pagans and philosophers. Even those skilled in the Law of Moses were unable to comprehend it, it being invisible and of such profundity that it far exceeds all human and angelic capacity to grasp. In this mortal life we believe it because faith teaches it to us, but in Heaven we will see it, and this will constitute part of our eternal felicity. Other miracles clustered around the Incarnation; one of the greatest is that the divine Word was conceived and born of a woman who was at once both Mother and Virgin. Many marvels accompanied the birth of the Saviour, as the appearance of the star which brought the Magi from the East. [*Matt.* 2:1-2]. But although these signs were done to manifest Our Lord's glory, it was not He who wrought them, but the Father and the Holy Spirit. Certainly, as God, He wrought them also, for what the Father does, so do the Son and the Holy Spirit as well. But as to the miracle of Cana, it is properly the Son who wrought it.

Here is a second difficulty. Many ancient Fathers assert the probable truth that our divine Lord performed many miracles while He lived in Egypt and in His parents' house. But these, too, were very secret and invisible, because Our Lord was not known at that time. Thus, the sign of Cana in Galilee, of which the Evangelist speaks, was truly the first which He performed to manifest His glory.

But what reflection shall we make as a consolation which our faith gives? Note that this first miracle was wrought by changing water into wine, just as the last wrought by Jesus Christ in His mortal sojourn was the changing of wine into His Blood in the Most Holy Sacrament of the Eucharist. We preachers of God's word are obliged to speak of each mystery as it is celebrated and to draw consolations from our faith. Today I will treat of the consolation which comes to us from our faith in the Eucharist. I am not going to teach you, for you believe it and are well established and confirmed in your belief, even willing to die upholding this truth. Rather than teach you, I am going to fill your heart with joy and consolation derived from speaking of these great mysteries.

Our Lord is the First, the Alpha and the Omega [*Apoc.* (*Rev.*) 1:8; 22:13], the Beginning and the End of all things. To represent this truth about Divinity and to make it better understood, the Egyptians painted a serpent biting its tail. This made the serpent appear to be round, with neither beginning nor end; his head, which was the beginning, was touching the end, which was his tail. So Our Lord, who from all eternity is the Beginning of all things, will be the End of them for all eternity. He has always made the beginning like the end, a marvelous correspondence between the two. When God created Adam, the first sign of that creation was changing mud into a human body. Likewise, when Jesus Christ re-created, the first sign of this re-creation was the transformation of one substance into another, the changing

of water into wine. Yes, the Saviour came to re-create what
was lost. "I will come," He said, "to make a new man."
Man was so destroyed by sin that he no longer appeared to
be what he had been originally. That is why, to renew him,
Our Lord began his re-creation as He had done his creation.
What a marvelous correspondence! In the creation of man,
God changed earth into human flesh, an amazing transformation. After saying: Let Us make man to Our image and likeness, He took some clay and shaped it into a body which
was still only a mass of earth. Then He breathed into this
body, and the mass was changed into flesh and blood; He
made of it a living man. [*Gen.* 1:26-27; 2:7]. Something similar
occurs in the re-creation. Our Lord begins by transforming
water into wine, giving this sign to reveal His glory.

He always manifests this correspondence in all His works.
Look at Him at the moment of His entrance into the world.
He was born quite naked from His Mother's womb. According to the revelations of St. Bridget, the most holy Virgin
found Him naked before her eyes, having given birth to this
most blessed Fruit without labor and without prejudice to
her virginity. She being absorbed in a gentle, loving and comforting contemplation, the Saviour came forth unnoticed from
her womb. Coming out of her rapture, she saw Him there
quite naked. She took Him and wrapped Him in swaddling
clothes and little woolens. He chose to leave this world as
He had entered it, dying quite naked on the tree of the Cross.
After His death He was taken down, allowing Himself to
be shrouded in swathing bands as He had done at His Nativity. He was born crying, just as all other infants. All are
born crying; the only exception, according to Pliny, was
Zoroaster, a very wicked man who and was "born laugh-
ing"! But Our Lord was born crying and wailing, as the Book
of Wisdom testifies: Although a great and wonderful king,
I was born, like all children, crying and wailing. [*Wis.* 7:3].
Though it really refers to Solomon, the passage may readily
be applied to Our Lord. Thus our true Solomon, though born
sovereign King of the earth, yet willed to be born weeping,

and accordingly to die weeping.

He chose to begin the Gospel by this first sign of the changing of water into wine. He chose to end His ministry of preaching by changing wine into Blood. He performed the first miracle at a banquet, and the last, the Eucharist, at another banquet. He changed water into wine at the wedding feast of Cana, and at the Last Supper, which was as the wedding feast of this Sacred Spouse, He transformed bread into His Flesh and wine into His Blood; with this transubstantiation He began to solemnize those nuptials which He consummated on the tree of the Cross. For the day of the Saviour's death was the day of His marriage. [Cf. *Cant.* 3:11].

In brief, in His first miracle He changed water into wine; and in the last one which He performed before His death He instituted the Eucharist, the Sacrament of His true presence. We believe this truth and this mystery which, along with the Incarnation, is the greatest and most hidden of all. Because faith teaches it, we believe that Jesus Christ is in this Most Holy Sacrament, body and soul. The Apostle says that the Christian is nourished with the living Flesh and Blood of the living God [*1 Cor.* 10:16; 11:24-27], and this is true. This truth may contradict our senses, which perceive nothing of its reality. Yet we believe it—and even believe it with greater delight the more our senses fail us here. Because of the hidden nature of the sacred mystery of the Eucharist, Divine Providence has provided us with thousands of proofs of this truth in hundreds of places, both in the Gospel and in the Old Testament. Our Lord Himself has so enlightened the understanding of some who have written on this subject that it is sheer delight to hear about and read what they have written so clearly and intelligently. Certainly we ought to make a thousand adorations each day to this divine Sacrament in thanksgiving for the love with which God dwells among us. These reflections ought to be a great consolation derived from this mystery of our faith.

Let us now turn to the question of how this miracle was wrought. For this I shall relate the whole of the Gospel story.

There was, says St. John, a wedding at Cana in Galilee. This was a small town near Nazareth where the relatives of the Virgin and Our Lord lived. They had a wedding, to which the Saviour and His Mother had been invited. Some Doctors delight in discussing whether the Apostles were there as invited guests or not. It is amazing how many different opinions there are on this subject. Let us bypass these arguments and follow what the Evangelist says. Besides, many of the ancient Fathers think that since Our Lord and His most holy Mother were invited, for their sake the Apostles were invited as well. St. John says quite clearly: and His disciples. We must follow that view. It is questioned whether this wedding feast was that of St. John or of another; but let us pass over that, it matters little. In any event, our dear Master and Our Lady were invited. They went; but when? Oh, certainly, it is likely that the holy Virgin arrived the evening before. For the women and relatives arrived on the eve of a wedding feast, not only to be received but also to assist in receiving the other guests, and in this way to pay honor to the bride. This holy Lady, who was extremely humble, certainly must have gone the evening before to render this kind service to the bride and bridegroom.

The Apostles went to this wedding feast, and Our Lord did not refuse the invitation either. For, you see, He had come to buy back, to re-form and to re-create man. He did not choose to do this with a demeanor that was grave, austere and rigid, but one that was most kind, polite and altogether courteous. Thus, being invited, He did not excuse Himself, but went, and His presence lessened some of the excessive frivolity and revelry usually found on such occasions. Certainly the weddings at which Our Lord and Our Lady are present are well-ordered and display great moderation.[2] The contrary is true with many of ours today. They are often full of frivolity and even deceptions. When one plans a daughter's marriage, how many falsehoods are spoken! She is this, she is that, she has so much inheritance; this young man has such and such rank and qualities. And on this basis they conclude the marriage, only to discover that much that was said is not the case at all. Then regrets and reproaches come, and on both sides. But it is too late for that, for the marriage is made. The marriage of Cana was not like this at all, for there is no deceit where Our Lord is. How modest this feast must have been, with the Saviour's presence causing great restraint.

Now I cannot imagine how it happened, but the wine began to fail. The servants grew a bit anxious in seeing the bottles emptying and made note of it among themselves while pouring the wine. Perhaps in this way it reached the ears of the women, who then began to make plans to address the problem. The all-holy Virgin, who was wise, prudent and full of charity, conceived an admirable expedient to relieve the embarrassment. But what will this holy Lady do, for she carries no money with which to buy wine? Her Son has none. How does she expect to help these people in their need? Oh, indeed, she knows she has with her the One who is all-powerful and whose great charity and kindness are very familiar to her. His all-powerful kindness will unfailingly provide for these poor people in their need.

It is very likely that it was a marriage of poor people. For this reason Our Lord was invited. In truth, He delighted in dealing with the poor and being with them. He always favored them. More often than not He was found among them; He loved poverty everywhere, even in kings' palaces, and particularly delighted in being in the midst of poverty. If our dear Saviour so delights in finding poverty in the houses of the great and at wedding feasts, what will be His delight to find it in religious houses where a vow is made to observe it![3] His delight will be to find frugality there in the midst of sufficiency, not the absence of necessities, but the absence of superfluities. Let this little instruction be said in passing.

The Virgin approaches her Son who alone, without money, can meet this need. Notice what this most holy Lady does and says: My Lord, they have no more wine. It is as if she meant to say: "My Lord and my Son, these people here are poor, and although poverty is extremely lovable and greatly pleasing to You, yet it is often a shameful experience, reducing one to the world's scorn and derision. These good people, Your hosts, will experience great shame if You do not help them. I know that You are all-powerful and will provide for their necessity and keep them from shame and humiliation. I never doubt Your charity and kindness. Keep in mind the hospitality they have extended to us—inviting us to their banquet. Please provide them with what they need."

The holy Virgin did not need to make a long case to her Son of this couple's needs. Skilled in the art of praying, she used the shortest but most excellent way of praying, saying only these words: My Son and my Lord, they have no more wine. By these words this sacred Virgin says "You are so kind and charitable, Your Heart is so merciful and full of pity; please grant me what I ask You for these poor people." A most excellent prayer, certainly, one in which this holy Lady speaks to Our Lord with the greatest reverence and humility imaginable. She goes to her Son not with assurance, nor with presumption, as some dare to do, but with a most profound humility, with which she presents to Him this couple's needs, convinced that He will provide for them.

Thus, it is a very good prayer simply to present one's needs to Our Lord, place them before the eyes of His goodness, and leave it to Him to act as He sees fit, convinced that He will answer us according to our needs. When, for example, we find ourselves dry, desolate and disheartened, let us follow the Virgin's example and say to Him, "Lord, look on me here, poor daughter that I am, desolate, afflicted, full of dryness and aridities." "See me here, Lord, poor man that I am, the poorest of all men and full of sins." "But what do you want?" "Oh, what do I want? You know well what I need; it is enough for me to present myself to You as I am. You will provide for my miseries and necessities as You see fit."

Certainly one can pray not only for spiritual, but for temporal things as well. That can and ought to be done, since

Our Lord Himself taught us to do so. In the Lord's Prayer we ask daily that God's Kingdom come (it being the beginning and end for which we live), and then that His will be done, that will being the sole means to that beatitude. But besides that, we make another request, namely, that He give us our daily bread. [*Matt.* 6:9-13; *Lk.* 11:2-4]. Holy Church even has special prayers by which we ask God for temporal favors, such as prayers for peace in time of war, for rain in time of drought, and for fair weather in time of too much rain. Indeed, there are even special Masses for times of plagues. The point is absolutely clear: we can and ought to ask God for both our spiritual and temporal needs.

There are two ways of asking things of Our Lord. The first is to pray as the Virgin prayed; the other is more specific, asking for such and such a thing or that He deliver us from some evil, always under the condition that it be according to His will, not ours. [*Lk.* 22:42]. But ordinarily we do not implore Him so specifically. You may come across a person who is wholly committed to piety and who, in all her prayers, asks for great consolation. What do you request, my dear daughter? I ask for consolations. Yes, that is good. But I ask also for humility, for I am not humble, yet I see that one can do nothing without that dear virtue. I also ask for the love of God, which renders everything so light and easy. It is good to ask for humility. This ought to be our most treasured virtue. And it is a good thing to ask and long for divine love. Yet, I assure you that your request for humility and love is not as good as it ought to be. For do you not see that you do not really desire humility, but only the feeling of humility? You wish to feel that you are humble, and, with that feeling, to know you have it. This must not be done, for to have this virtue it is not necessary to have its feeling. On the contrary, those who are truly humble are not really aware of being so. Likewise, to love God it is not necessary to feel that love, for love of God does not consist in feeling, tasting and enjoying His consolations. You can be very humble and love God very much without feeling so.

"Oh, that I might love God like a St. Catherine of Siena, or a St. Teresa." You are deceiving yourself: say more honestly that you wish to have the ecstasies, the feelings of love and humility of a St. Teresa or a St. Catherine of Siena, for it is not love that you want, but its consoling feeling. It is only the lack of feelings of which we complain, for we wish to taste and relish everything. O God, wait a little, my dear souls. Here below is not the place for tastes and feelings. Wait till you are in Heaven above, where you will experience humility and enjoy its sweetness. You will see then how much you love God, and will taste the consoling sweetness of His love. But in this life the Lord wills us to live between fear and hope, to be humble and love Him without necessarily feeling either.[4]

Let us return to the most holy Virgin: My Lord, she says, they have no more wine. The Lord answers her: "Woman, what have you to do with Me? My hour is not yet come." This answer may seem at first to be a bit harsh.[5] To hear such a Son speak in this way to such a Mother! To hear so gentle and kind a Son reject His Mother's request so brusquely, her prayer made with so much reverence and humility! What words between Son and Mother, between the two most loving and lovable hearts that ever were! "What have you to do with Me, woman?"

Ah, Lord, what has the creature to do with her Creator, from whom she has received being and life? What has the Mother to do with the Son? What has the Son to do with the Mother, from whom He received His body, that is, His humanity of flesh and blood! These words seem to be very strange, and have been frequently misunderstood by those attempting to interpret them. Such misunderstanding has given rise to several heresies! One would be bold indeed to attempt with the understanding alone, and without divine help, to grasp the true meaning of these words. The truth is that this was a very loving response, one fully understood as such by the holy Virgin. With it, she felt herself the most obliged of all mothers. She made it clear that she grasped its true

meaning and was fully confident when she said to the servers:
"You have heard my Son's answer, but because you do not
understand love's language, you may consider it a refusal.
Not at all. Just do whatever He tells you, and do not be
anxious about anything. Assuredly He will address your
needs."

There are many diverse opinions among the Doctors on
these words: Woman, what have you to do with Me? Some
say that He meant this: "What have you and I to worry about?
We are only guests and ought not to have to be concerned
about such things," and many similar interpretations. But let
us hold firm to what the majority of the Fathers hold—that
the Saviour used these words to His holy Mother to teach
persons holding some high Church position, such as bishops,
not to use their offices to favor their blood relations, or to
favor them in any way contrary to God's law. They ought
never on their relatives' account to forget their dignity and
abandon the uprightness with which they are obliged to exercise
their offices.

Our divine Master desired to give this lesson to the world
and used the heart of the most holy Virgin for this purpose.
In this He actually gives her a very great proof of His love.
He meant this: "My dear Mother, in replying 'What have
you to do with Me?' I in no way intend to refuse your request" (for what can such a Son refuse to the most loving
and loved Mother ever?). "You have loved Me perfectly, and
I have loved you sovereignly. This love we have for one another permits Me to take advantage of your heart's constancy
as I teach this lesson to the world. I am certain that your
most loving heart will not take offense. Although it may appear a little harsh to others, it does not appear so to you,
who understand the language of love." Love does not express
itself only by words, but also by the eyes, gestures and actions. For instance, tears which flow from prayer are often
proof of our love, as the Psalmist gave witness when he poured
forth abundant tears before God. [*Ps.* 6:7; 38(39):13; 41(42):4;
55(56):9].

The spouse in the Canticle of Canticles said: "My Beloved is for me a bundle of myrrh; I will take Him and place Him between my breasts" [*Cant.* 1:12(13)], that is to say, in the midst of my affections; "and a drop of this myrrh will strengthen and comfort my heart." So this divine lover,[6] the most sacred Virgin, takes the words of Our Lord as a bundle of myrrh and puts them between her breasts, in the midst of her love; she receives the drop that flows from this myrrh. It so strengthens her heart that, hearing the reply which to others seemed a refusal, she believed without a doubt that the Saviour had granted her what she had asked of Him. So she confidently says to the attendants: Do whatever He tells you.

As for the words, "My hour is not yet come," some thought that Our Lord meant that the wine had not yet failed. There are many other interpretations and opinions of the holy Fathers on this subject, but I do not wish to dwell upon them. It is true that there are special moments ordained by Divine Providence for us and on which depend all our good and our conversion. It is also true that God had determined from all eternity the hour and moment of effecting two great miracles, that of the Incarnation and that of giving to the world this first sign to manifest His glory. But this divine will was not so bound that Our Lord could not advance that moment when asked by His Mother.

To understand this better, remember the example of Rebecca and Isaac, who both desired to have children. Unfortunately, Rebecca was sterile and, according to the laws of nature, could not have any. Yet from all eternity God had foreseen and ordained that Rebecca would conceive and have children—but on the condition that she be granted them by her prayers. Thus if she had not prayed for them with her husband Isaac, she would not have conceived. Realizing that they were childless because of her sterility, she and her husband shut themselves up in a room and prayed so fervently that God heard them, granted their prayer, and Rebecca became pregnant with the twins Esau and Jacob [*Gen.* 25:21].

In just this way, the loving sighs of Our Lady advanced the Incarnation of Our Lord, according to the ancient Doctors. It is not that He became incarnate before the time that He had foreordained. No. But in His eternity He had foreseen that the holy Virgin would implore Him to hasten the moment of His coming into the world, and that He would hearken to her prayer and become incarnate sooner than He would have if she had not prayed.

It is quite the same with this first miracle that Our Lord worked today at the wedding feast of Cana. "My hour is not yet come," He said to His holy Mother, "but since I can refuse you nothing, I will advance this hour to do what you ask." From all eternity He had foreseen that He would anticipate it in favor of Our Lady's prayers. Oh, how blessed is the hour of Divine Providence in which God has willed to bestow on us so many graces and blessings. Oh, how blessed is the soul who will await that hour with patience and who will prepare herself to respond with fidelity to it when it comes. Certainly that was the hour of Divine Providence in which the Samaritan woman was converted. Likewise, on this hour of Divine Providence our conversion and reformation depend; and we ought to take diligent care to be well-disposed for it, so that when Our Lord comes, we will be ready to respond wholeheartedly to His grace.

The Saviour commanded the attendants to fill six stone water jars that were set there for the purifying of the Jews, since they always washed when they had touched something forbidden by the Law. They had rigid exterior ceremonies to which they were extremely exact, but according to Scripture they took scarcely any care to purify their interior. [*Matt.* 23:25-26; *Mk.* 7:3-6]. (I have seen one of these jars in Paris in a house of the religious of the Cistercian Order. It was very large, as is the Hebrew style, but I did not measure it because I saw it only from a distance.) These attendants were very careful to do as the sacred Virgin directed them, for as soon as the command was given they filled these jars so full that, according to the sacred text, the water overflowed.

Then Our Lord said an interior word which no one heard, and immediately all the water was changed into very good wine. This word was doubtless similar to that which He used when He created all things from nothing and gave life and being to man, and which He used in that last banquet with His disciples when He changed the wine into His Blood in the Most Holy Sacrament of the Eucharist. And what an exceptionally excellent wine! By it we are nourished, in that it is by the reception of the Body and Blood of the Saviour that the merits of His Passion and Death are applied to us.

Ordinarily kings and great princes always carry with them powder from the horns of the unicorn, which serves as a protection against poison. When they have some indisposition they take some of this powder in wine to preserve their health. The human spirit is amazing! Many question the existence of unicorns and whether the powder from their horns has this efficacy. To go seeking for reasons for such arguments is not to our point. For the present, let us follow those who say that there are unicorns and that their powder has the property of counteracting poison.[7] All can have this powder, not only princes. Nevertheless these latter have this advantage over others: their goblets, in which they put the powder from the unicorn, are made from the unicorn's horn. The Precious Blood of Our Lord is like the unicorn, expelling the venom of sin, which is poisonous to our souls. By the Sacrament of the Eucharist, the fruit of our Redemption is applied to us, as we have just said. This Sacrament was prefigured by miracles wrought in the Old Law. For instance, Moses had a rod by which he wrought marvelous and frightening things, for it was changed into a serpent and adder; and then, when he desired, it became a rod again. He used it to make water flow out of the rock [Ex. 17:5-6] and to change the waters into blood. [Ex. 7:19-20]. In short, he worked prodigies which were figures of those which were to happen in the law of grace. [Cf. 1 Cor. 10:4, 11].

Let us conclude by saying a word about Our Lady's power to present our needs before her Son. We must invite her to our banquet too, since where the Son and Mother are the wine will not fail. She will infallibly say: "My Lord, this daughter of mine has no more wine." But, my dear souls, for what wine do you ask? "Oh, certainly, that of consolation. It is all that we desire." A simple example will make this clear. A good woman has a sick son who is also her only child. She cries out to God: "He is the fruit of my womb; in him I have put all my hope." And when human remedies can do no more, she has recourse to vows made to the saints.[8] All this is of course good: it is right to invoke the saints. But, my dear daughter, why do you so beg for your son's health? When he is well, what will you do with him? "I will put him on the altar of my heart and burn incense before him." Now do you not see? If the Virgin had asked for wine so that those at the wedding could become inebriated, Our Lord would not have changed the water into wine.[9]

If we want Our Lady to ask her Son to change the water of our tepidity into the wine of His love, we must do whatever He tells us. This is a good point. Those attendants were extremely prompt in accomplishing all that He commanded them, as our divine Mistress had counseled them. Let us do well what the Saviour tells us: let us fill our hearts with the water of penitence, and this tepid water will be changed into the wine of fervent love. Do carefully what is at hand today, and tomorrow you will be ordered to do something else.

Do we wish to have a long and fervent prayer? Let us nourish ourselves with good thoughts during the day, making frequent ejaculatory prayers. Do you wish to be recollected in prayer? Outside of prayer keep yourself as if you were there, and do not waste time in useless reflections, either on yourself or on what happens around you. Do not amuse yourself with trifles. You would wish to have some light of faith to understand the mystery of the Incarnation? Nourish yourself the whole day long with pious thoughts on the infinite goodness of our God.

Finally, my dear Sisters, practice well what you have been

taught until now, and rest in the providence of God; for He will never fail to supply what is necessary to you. [*Ps.* 54(55):23; *1 Ptr.* 5:7]. Praise Him in this life, and you will glorify Him with all the blessed in Heaven. May the Father, the Son and the Holy Spirit lead us there! Amen.

NOTES

1. *Luke* 12:35-40, for the Feast of St. Antony, Abbot.
2. Cf. *Introduction to the Devout Life,* Part III, chap. 38.
3. Cf. *Sermons for Lent,* "God's Spiritual Providence," March 6, 1622, p. 125.
4. St. Francis de Sales did a great deal of spiritual direction and was aware firsthand of how often people confuse the feeling of a certain virtue with its reality. He frequently insists on the distinction, as here, in order to encourage realism in the devout life. Holiness does not consist in consoling feelings, nor in raptures and ecstasies. It consists rather in doing God's will generously, zealously and perseveringly, no matter whether with such feelings or without. This teaching came frequently from St. Francis.
5. Cf. *Sermons for Lent,* "Proper Fear of Death," March 10, 1622, pp. 139-140.
6. As elsewhere in St. Francis' sermons, we have here capitalized the words "Lover," "Beloved," and "Spouse" when they refer to Our Lord and made them lower case when they refer to Our Lady, the Church, or the faithful soul. The word "divine" is not always to be taken in the literal sense of referring to God Himself.
7. Always keep in mind that St. Francis will use any suitable example to convey his spiritual point—even, as here, the mythical unicorn.
8. Cf. *Treatise on the Love of God,* end of Preface; *Introduction to the Devout Life,* Part III, chap. 23.
9. The point seems a bit obscure at first. The mother in the example wants her son's health returned so she can, in a sense, "worship" him. Since this is against God's will, her prayer is unworthy. It would be like Our Lady asking for the miracle at Cana so that people could get drunk. St. Francis' point is this: pray, yes, but only for what is good.

INDEX
Topical Index

Abraham 85
Adam/Eve
    and circumcision........... 89
    creation of.... 85, 105-106, 116
    human behavior after fall of
    76-77
    "like God" by knowledge of
        good and evil..... 21, 22, 24
    Original Justice............ 21
        forfeited............ 21, 23
        might not have been lost
            if Adam asked pardon.... 4
        never sinned in........... 24
        questioned by God......... 3-4
        seduced by pride and ambition
        .... 20-21, 24
        tempted by Lucifer...... 20-21
        tempter disguised himself
            in tempting............. 22
Alexander the Great.......... 52
Ambrose, St.
    on humility 24-25
        miracle at Cana........ 104
    virtues of.............. 17-18
Ancient Fathers
    morning star (Mary),
        kept their sights on....... 53
    on Adam's non-acknowledge-
        ment of sin.............. 4
    on Christ
        praise of Baptist by..... 16
        titles of
            "Desire of the eternal
            hills"........ 25-26, 63
            "Desired of the Na-
            tions"....... 25-26, 63
            essential 100
    on circumcision........ 89, 95
        Isaias 40:1-4............ 41

Ancient Fathers (cont.)
    on John the Baptist, St.
        denials by 28
        sends disciples to
            Jesus 2-3
        why he questioned Our
            Lord 2-3
    manna........... 54-55, 69
    miracle at Cana
        .... 104, 108, 113
    miracles of Jesus in Egypt
        and Nazareth......... 105
    nepotism 113
    questions—reasons for... 2-3
    Scribes, Pharisees question-
        ing the Baptist...... 23-24
Angels
    address St. Joseph.......... 65
    at Nativity............. 65, 85
    can speak about God far
        better than we........... 84
    cannot weep.............. 4-5
    "eternal hills" are...... 25, 63
    Incarnation
        cannot comprehend...... 104
        desired by Angels........ 25
        represent the............. 64
        inspiration from............ 96
        made the manna.......... 70
        question Magdalen........... 4
        sing and speak to shepherds
        .... 5, 56, 85
Angels, bad. See Lucifer.
Anna...................... 60
Anthony, St.—on humility..... 32
Asceticism. See Spiritual life;
    Circumcision, spiritual.
Augustine, St............. 17, 83
Beatific Vision in Christ... 77, 89

Bishops and priests
    duties of........10, 37-38, 46
    election or call of..........37
    spiritual circumcision of..91-93
    symbolized by shepherds....56
    titles of engraved in heart
       100-101
Blandina, St.................11
Blood, Precious..............50
    and Name of Jesus88, 99-100, 102
    payment of our debts.......99
    shed as a deposit...........99
            Saviour............99
            out of love...........99
Bonaventure, St..............68
Bridget, St.—vision of the
    Nativity 106
Cana, Wedding Feast
    of...103-105, 108-110, 112-116
    first miracle of Our Lord
        ....103, 104
        advanced in favor of Our
            Lady's prayer.....114-115
        effected by an
            interior word..........116
        in return for hospitality...110
        properly wrought by
            the Son..............105
        purpose: manifest His glory
            ....103, 104, 105, 106
    Jewish customs at.....108, 115
    Our Lady's understanding of
        Jesus' words at......112-114
    presence of Christ restrained
        frivolity at..........108-109
    response of Jesus to
        Our Lady at........112-113
Catechism in novitiates........68
Christian—criteria of a true....11
Christians, early—fervor of.77-78
Chrysostom, St.
    on circumcision............89
        Jesus' response to
            Baptist's disciples......10

Chrysostom, St. (cont.)
    on questions, why posed......3
        St. Paul..............8-9
Circumcision. See also Blood.
    distinguishing mark of people
        of God.................89
    figure of spiritual
        circumcision.............88
    Jesus' willing submission to
        ....88-89, 99
        example for us...........99
    on part most damaged by sin.89
    "Sacrament" of Old Law, a.88
    like profession of faith in
        Our Lord's coming.....88
    made children of God.....88
    purification by from
        Original Sin...........88
Circumcision, spiritual
    binding on all.............91
    for our own benefit........99
    greater obligation of bishops,
        priests, religious
        to perform........91, 92-93
    mark of God's children.....92
    of heart, tongue, passions
        ....88-91, 95
    performed by someone else
       95-96
        made with more insight....96
        more meritorious......95-96
    rather than mere incision
        ....91-92, 95
    self-circumcision
        of ancient solitaries....95-96
Commandments (Law of God)
    observance of.......11, 12, 92
Confidence in God........45-46
Congregation of oblates
    Holy Family is a...........65
    Visitation Sisters...........63
Conversion
    in hour of Providence......115
    interior................11, 39

Conversion (cont.)
of David, King.........43-45
Paul, St................43
Samaritan woman.......115
putting off what is
useful for our..........39
Correction, fraternal....13, 95-96
Correspondences among God's
works..................105
banquet: scene of Jesus' first
and last miracles.......107
born naked/died naked.....106
born weeping/died weeping
...................106-107
creation: earth into flesh/
re-creation: water into
wine..............105-106
ministry of preaching began:
water into wine/ministry ended:
wine into Blood.....105-107
miracle, first: water into wine/
miracle, last before death:
instituted Eucharist.......107
swaddled in birth/shrouded
in death................106
wedding feasts: water into
wine/bread and wine into
His Body and Blood.....107
Creation. See also Adam.
by an interior word of
Our Lord:
day of creation..........116
Holy Eucharist..........116
miracle at Cana.........116
purpose: the Incarnation.....83
Cross, Tree of..........55, 107
in our life only gate to
Heaven 14-15
source of scandal........14-15
Cupid, portrayed as blind.....11
Cyrus................40-41, 45
David, King
fall and conversion.......43-45
penitence of...............18

Devil. See Lucifer and
bad angels.
Dina....................97-98
Divinity. See also Incarnation;
God; Hypostatic Union.
represented by circular
serpent 105
unknown by humanity.......71
Doctors of the Church
on Cana........104, 108, 113
circumcision............95
Our Lady's prayer
advancing Incarnation..115
passions................94
response of Our Lord to
Baptist................9
Elias 27-28
Emmaus.....................4
Equivocation 29
Eucharist, Holy
and Incarnation..........69-70
miracle at Cana
..........105, 107, 116
faith in..............105, 107
instituted out of love...56, 107
merits of Passion and Death
applied to us through
...............(2 refs.) 116
proofs of................107
Real Presence............107
thanksgiving for...........107
transubstantiation..........107
Eusebius....................11
"Evil generation"............42
Faith
in Holy Eucharist.....105, 107
Incarnation.....64, 104, 117
mystery of virginity......64
of John the Baptist......2, 5, 7
Shepherds 56
Virgin Mary..........114
Feast Days
in the Church 82, 88
Old Law................82

Feast Days (cont.)
  purpose of..............50,88
  vigils of
    in the Church..50-51, 63, 82
          Old Law.......51, 82
    keeping, as spiritual
      circumcision...........90
Gabriel, Angel 70
Gedeon...............74-75, 77
God
  acts of "ad extra"
  ....68-69, 104-105
  attribution:
    power to the Father.......69
    wisdom to the Son........69
    goodness to the Holy Spirit
   69
  communicated Himself in
    Incarnation 42
  creative act of Incarnation...69
  does will of those who do
    His will.................77
  exalts the humble....33-34, 47
  Father
    eternally begets the Son.83-84
    sole origin of Trinity......84
    Virgin of virgins.........84
  foreseen will of conditioned
    by prayer...........114-115
  goodness of
    and understanding of
      Incarnation 117
    in becoming incarnate.....42
      bestowing His graces...42
      making Jesus
        our brother..........85
      pardoning offences.....42
      rewarding magnanimously
     42
  has no equal...........21, 24
  Heart of......15, (3 refs.) 43
  Holy Spirit
    came upon Virgin Mary
      at Incarnation..........84

God (cont.)
  Holy Spirit (cont.)
    descends as a dove.......2
    goodness attributed to.....69
    in bosom of the Virgin 64
    rejects the proud........14
    sent to poor...........13-14
    united Divinity to humanity
      in Mary's womb.......85
  humbles the proud....33, 46-47
  immutable.................51
  just, infinitely..............47
  justice of. See Justice of God.
  light, God is..............52
  mercy of. See Mercy of God.
  omniscient...........3, 5, 69
  One in Three Persons.......69
  only means of finding........5
  penetrates the heart........46
  voice of Sts. John, Paul..36-37
  wrath of..................42
Gods, days named after pagan
 87-88
Gospel
  preached by the poor 13, 14
        to the poor.....13, 14
Grace
  and free will..............49
  disposes for a new grace....42
  fidelity to, importance of....42
  knowledge of one's misery...11
  never lacking to us........42
Gregory, St.................82
Heaven, enjoyment of..18, 93-94
Hebrew language.............30
Hell
  eternal punishment..........23
  greatest pain in............40
  on earth..............21, 23
Hemor...................97-98
Hilary, St.
  on Jesus' response to Baptist's
    disciples 10
    questions—reasons for.....3

Holy Orders, call to 37
Human nature
  body, origin of 70
  elevated above angelic
    nature 21
  soul, origin of 70-71
  two "natures":
    concupiscible . . .12, 26-27, 58
    irascible 12, 58
  union of body and soul in one
    indivisible person 72-73
Humility. See also Jesus Christ;
Mary, Blessed Virgin;
  John the Baptist.
  affinity of with charity . . .31-32
  and confidence 46
  engendered by poverty 13
  exalted by God 33-34
  feeling of 111-112
  first degree of 27
  from knowing our misery—
    sign of interior conversion. 11
  humble receive the Spirit of
    Christ 13, 34
  loved by Christ 13
  most necessary virtue 31-32
  necessary for combat against
    vice 24-25
  precursor of charity 32
  preferred by God 33-34
  publican's 47
  St. Anthony's vision on 32
Incarnation 21, 26
  accomplished at Virgin's
    "fiat" 71, 84
  and Eucharist 69-70
    faith 64, 104, 114-115
  Beatific Vision of
    Our Lord 77, 89
  celebrated in Heaven 80
  desired by angels 25
           God 26
  desired/known by Patriarchs
    and Prophets 26, 51-52

Incarnation (cont.)
  desired/known by humankind
    in general 26, 51-52
  divinity sustains humanity in.75
  glory made possible for us
    by .53
  God's desire for, communicated
    beforehand to angels and
    men 26
  greater gift than manna 53
  Holy Spirit came upon the
    Virgin in 84
  hour of advanced by prayer of
    Our Lady 114-115
  human characteristics taken
    on by God in 72
  hypostatic union in. See Hypo-
    static Union.
  joy of Heaven, will constitute
    part of our 104
  "kiss" in Canticle of
    Canticles, signified by 26
  manna symbolizes. See
    Symbols—manna.
  marriage with human nature. 107
  mercy, great revelation of
    God's
    accomplished when evil was
      at its height 42
    motivated solely by
      His own goodness 42
  miracle of miracles 104
  moment of determined from
    all eternity 114
  mystery uniquely Christian . . .51
  purpose of creation 83
  purpose: make us share
    Christ's glory 85
  purpose: to teach by example
      . . . . . . .57-58, 76-78, 85, 89
    man's gratitude for 76
  Son alone became incarnate
    .68-69
  splendor of blinds our minds.52

Incarnation (cont.)
  suffering and sorrow of,
    foreseen and embraced
    in love 77-78
  unforeseen by pagans and
    philosophers 104
  union of divine and human
    natures in. See also Jesus
    Christ—hypostatic union in.
    . . . . 71-72, 73-76
  union of Jesus' will
    with the Father's will 77
  work of all Three Persons
    . . . . 68-69, 70-71, 104-105
              Trinity alone 70
Inspirations 42, 96, 114
Isaias
  interpretations of 40:1-4 . . 41-45
  prophecies of 40
Israelites
  in captivity 40
    desert 38-39, 51, 54
Jacob
  blessing of Joseph 63
  in Sichem 97-99
  Messianic prophecy of . . . 25, 63
  prophecy of exile 41
Jepthe 101
Jesus Christ
  Abraham's seed, of 85
  circumcision of 88-89
  complete detachment of . . . 77-78
  conformity of His will to
    Father's will 77
  death day was day of His
    marriage 107
  demeanor of 108
  divinity of, proofs of 85
  equal to the Father 59, 84
  equanimity of spirit of 48
  eyes of
    gentle 80
    gracious and benign 59
    simple glance of 61

Jesus Christ (cont.)
  great penances, did not
    perform 7, 16
  humanity of
    creation of 85
    possessed every grace and
      blessing 88-89
    proof of 85
  humiliations of 14-15
  humility of 10, 22, 55, 80
  hypostatic union in
    . . . 21, 26, 51, 52, 55, 64, 69
    . . . . 71-76, 84, 88-89
    indissoluble in death 74-75
    makes humankind sharers in
      divinity 84
    not merited 55
    symbols of. See Symbols.
    work of God's Providence . 71
  in guise of gardener,
  in guise of pilgrim 4
  Incarnation of. See Incarnation.
  Infant
    and Bl. V. Mary 79-80
    gifts to 59
    gives different consolation
      to each visitor 59
    King of our faculties and
      senses 60
    "novice" in the
      Holy Family 65
    proofs of divinity of 85
    Salvation expected by
      all 63
        Mary 63-64
    silence of 65
    source of joy and happiness
      60
    subject to laws of infancy
      . . . . 57-59, 65, 85
    visitors to. See Persons—
      "four" kinds.
  Light inacessible 54
  love of for us 77-78

Jesus Christ (cont.)

Messias..........2, 6, 10, 23
miracles of. See Miracles.
model for our imitation
....55, 57-59, 62, 76-78, 85,
................89, 95, 99
Name of
    and Precious Blood.88, 99-100
    at moment of our death...102
    demons tremble at.......102
    given by Eternal Father..102
    how to pronounce it
    ....100, 101, 102
    means Saviour 99
    password to Heaven..100-102
    saves men..............102
nativity of. See Nativity of
    Our Lord.
obedience of...........57-59
omniscient..........5, 16, 59
omnipotent kindness of .109-110
our brother...............85
passible 71-72
Passion of accepted by at
    Incarnation..............78
poor and, the.........9, 13-14
poverty
    in Bethlehem 65, 79-80
    preferred........13-14, 109
praised St. John the Baptist
    ....15-16, 28-29
preached to the poor..9, 13, 14
proud, flees the 13-14
questioned disciples on way
    to Emmaus..............4
questioned Magdalen......4-5
Sacred Heart of. See Sacred
    Heart.
sinless....................88
Son of God...............7
    begotten.............54, 84
    brought forth............54
    virginally produced
    on earth........54, 70, 84

Jesus Christ (cont.)

sorrow and suffering of
    embraced from moment of
        Incarnation 77
    subject to.............77-78
soul of, inferior part of.
    See also hypostatic
    union in..............77-78
subject to His Mother.......58
titles of
    Alpha and Omega.......105
    Bread of Angels.......55-56
    Christ (High Priest,
        Anointed One) 100
    Desire of the eternal
        hills 25-26, 63
    Desired of the Nations
        ....25-26, 63
    Emmanuel...............63
    essential: Creator, Jesus,
        Supreme Being........100
    participated in by mankind:
        Christ and Saviour.....100
    Head of all creatures......85
    King and Legislator.......63
    Lamb of God............7
    Lord of creation..........85
    Saviour 99
    Shepherd, sovereign
        ....56, 59, 61
    Shepherd, a good.........57
    Truth...................16
union of with the Father.....77
use of reason from conception
   58
weeping..........85, 106,107
John the Baptist, St.
    ambition, resisted..........25
    and the Messias:
        adored Him while in womb .2
        consecrated to His service
            from the womb..........2
        faith in Him never wavered
            ....2, 5, 7

John the Baptist, St. (cont.)
and the Messias (cont.):
knowledge of Him.......2, 5
Incarnation ... 2
Precursor of...........2, 37
rejoiced in Him in womb...2
sent disciples 1
to be instructed by Him
personally........6, 7, 8
detach them from
himself 7
make Him known......5-7
voice of Our Lord....36, 37
constancy of............15-16
denied he was the Messias,
Elias, the Prophet
......25, 26, 28-29, 32, 33
denied without lying.....27-29
disciples of preferred him
to Christ..............7, 16
exalted by God.............33
humility of...22, 24, 25, 26-36
model for prelates, preachers,
religious 34
praised by Our Lord.....15-16
as an angel 33
a prophet 33
pupil of Our Lady...........2
sanctified in womb..........2
simplicity in responding
..............26, 27, 28-29
sinned (possibly), venially
................24, 25, 48
temptation of
by friends 23
nature of his.........22, 25
truth
imprisoned for 1
lover of................25
voice in the desert
...........31-33, 36-37, 45
John the Evangelist, St........36
possibly the groom at Cana
.... 108

Joseph, Patriarch.............63
Joseph, St...............60, 65
Justice of God.....42, 47, 77, 99
Leitmotif: Live Jesus........102
Libraries, and spiritual avarice.39
Love
feeling of 111-112
first passion of soul.........59
in well-ordered soul........18
of God for us..............98
our gift to Infant..........59
worldly..................98
Lucifer and bad angels
became devils.........22, 24
fall of through
arrogance, ambition.20-21, 24
self-complacency
or envy............21-22
gods, never sought to be....24
in Lucifer devils began to be.24
snares of devils.....22, 32, 61
tempted Adam and Eve
.... 20-21, 22
tempted by themselves......22
Lying......................29
Magdalen at empty tomb.......4
Magi...............56, 72, 85
Malchus...................97
Mankind—in image and
likeness of God...........106
Manna........38-39, 51, 52-53
prefigured Eucharist......69-70
symbol of Incarnation. See
Symbols—manna.
Marriages, worldly 108-109
Mary, Blessed Virgin
Abraham's race, member of..85
all-holy..................109
at Bethlehem.....59-60, 65, 80
blood of formed
Jesus' body 70-71
chosen for her virginity.....53
chosen from eternity........85
equanimity of spirit........48

Mary, Blessed Virgin (cont.)
  faith of, confident........114
  "fiat" and Incarnation......71
  heart of and Sacred Heart
   112-114
  humility of
    ....22, 33, 108, 110, 112
  intercessory power of..116-117
    condition: we do God's will
     117-118
    turns water of repentance,
      tepidity into wine of love
     117
  Magnificat of..............33
  Morning Star...........53, 54
  Most excellent creature......85
  Mother of the Son.........112
  Myrrh of the Sea...........64
  poverty of.................65
  prayer of
    advanced hour of first
      miracle...........114-115
    moment of Incarnation
     114-115
    at Cana.......109-112, 114
    Nativity..............106
  Star of the Sea
    guided Ancient Fathers,
      Patriarchs & Prophets...53
  teacher of the Baptist........2
  Virgin and Mother........104
  virginal
    in birth of Jesus
      ....53-54, 84-85, 106
    conception of Jesus
      ....52, 53, 70-71
  virginity/fecundity of........64
Mercy of God........41-43, 47
  infinite 47
  presumption on........46, 47
  revealed in Old Testament.41-42
  toward David 43-45
    St. Paul 43
    sinners.........43, 45

Miracles
  accompanying the Incarnation
   104-105
    star 104
    virgin conception, birth...104
  Cana. See Cana, wedding feast of.
  during hidden life 105
  Gospel preached to poor..9, 13
  in presence of Baptist's
    disciples.............7, 10
  of grace—cures of:
    spir. blindness...........11
    deafness...........13
    lameness........11-12
    leprosy 12-13
    death..............13
  of nature—cures of:
    blindness 11
    deafness 13
    lameness 11-12
    leprosy 12-13
    death...................13
  proof of the Messias.......23
  wrought by Our Lord to
    manifest His glory, the first
    .... 103, 104, 105, 106
  wrought by God to glorify
    Our Lord 104-105
Moses.....................51
Mysteries
  knowledge of for all
    Christians 67-68
  light of darkens our minds...52
  necessity of preparation for
    ....57, 64
Nathan....................44
Nativity of Our Lord. See
  also Jesus Christ—Infant;
  Incarnation.
  confirmed by signs.......5, 56
  consolation of granted
    according to the capacity of
    each individual
    ....57, 59-60, 64

Nativity of Our Lord (cont.)
  in darkness to lead us
    to glory 53
  mystery of
    and that of Visitation 59
    inexhaustible 51, 52
    uniquely Christian 51
    preparation for 57, 64-65
Nepotism 113
Oblates of the Visitation 63
Order and reason 18, 58, 59
Original Justice. See Adam;
  John the Baptist.
Original Sin 24
  and circumcision 88
  consequences of 4
  effects of on human behavior
    . . . . 76, 106
  penalty of might not have taken
    place if Adam had asked
    pardon 4
Paphnutius, St. 46
Pasch, Passage, Passover 82
Passions
  cannot be gotten rid of . . . 94-95
  heresy of Palestinian
    hermits on 94
  not sinful in themselves . . . 94-95
  struggle with until death . . 93-94
  victory in struggle against . . . 94
Passwords
  Jesus 100-102
  Scibboleth 101
Patriarchs and/or Prophets
  desired/knew the Incarnation
    . . . . 26, 52
  "eternal hills" 63
  "Morning Star," guided by . . 53
Paul, St.
  conversion of 43
  directed his spir. children
    to Christ 6
  discretion towards spir.
    children 8-9

Paul, St. (cont.)
  on almsgiving 89
  voice of God 36
Paula, St. 65
Penance, Sacrament of 30-31
Persons—"four" kinds:
  who do not wish to come to
    Christ 64
  who come for selfish reasons . 64
  who come to adore 59, 64
  who come to remain 60, 64
  who leave yet remain 64-65
Peter, St., poor—spiritual
  circumcision of 96-97
Pharisee and Publican 46-47
Poor hear Gospel 13-14
Poverty
  engenders humility 13
  extremely lovable 110
  in Bethlehem 65, 80
  in religious houses 109
  loved by Christ 13, 109
  sometimes humiliating 110
Prayer
  condition of foreseen will
    of God 114-115
  ecstasies in 15
  ejaculatory 5, 117
  for both spiritual and
    temporal favors 110-111
  intentions in, good and
    imperfect 117
  Lord's 111
  mental
    conditions for good 117
    knowledge is necessary
      for 67, 68
  of Isaac and Rebecca . . . 114-115
    petition 110-111
    praise . . 48, 59, 80, 102, 118
  Our Lady's power to present
    our needs to Jesus in . 116-117
  specific or general 111
  tears at 113

Prayer (cont.)
to Holy Trinity 61
Preachers, Teachers, Spir.
Directors
compared to angels......64-65
duties of..............37-38
necessary qualities of
discernment 9
discretion 8
zeal 9
principal aim: make God
known 5
should send pupils to Our
Lord's "school".........6-7
Present moment—its
importance 38-39
Priests. See Bishops and Priests.
Primitive Church.............50
Prophet, Great
promised in the Law
................27, 28, 36
Son of God, would be......28
Providence, Divine 39
and Holy Eucharist 107
Incarnation 71
conversion, ordains moments
of....................114
daily needs supplied by.39, 118
mercy of God......41-45, 47
obligations, imposes........38
trusting in 39, 118
Questions—why God asks.....3-5
that sins may be confessed..3-4
to enlighten 4
provoke love............4
Redemption
gate of Heaven, only.......99
infinite merit of any of
Christ's acts for......78, 99
joy in...................63
paid in full rigor of justice...78
price of our...........77-78
re-created what was lost
..................106-108

Redemption (cont.)
sufferings of, freely willed
by the Saviour...........78
Religious/Religious life
Bethlehem is 65
a desert...................15
hospital or sanatorium.......93
obedience in..............58
school of abnegation.....78-79
title of..............100-101
virtues of. See also
Spiritual life. 79
Sacraments. See also individual
Sacraments 11, 100
Sacred Heart of Jesus
and Heart of Mary........112
desired to shed His Blood for
us at Circumcision.......99
in Bethlehem 80
Incarnation revealed mercy
and kindness of........42-43
infinite merit of a single
sigh of..............78, 99
love of for us 77-78
mercy and kindness of
.... 42-43, 110
suffered from Conception....78
suffering willed by.......77-78
Scribes and Pharisees
almost lost patience with
the Baptist...............29
awaited the Messias......23-25
questioned the Baptist...23, 25
Shepherds
brought gifts...............59
simplicity of faith of........56
Sichem, circumcision of....98-99
Spirit of God 14
the world........14, 26
Spiritual children...........6-8
Spiritual directors, teachers,
etc. See Preachers.
Spiritual life
abnegation of all wills.......78

Spiritual life (cont.)
  abstinence 76-77
  almsgiving 89
  ambition, arrogance
    made a hell of earth 22-23
    originated in "heaven" 22
    powerful temptations . . . 20, 24
    resisted by Baptist 25
  avarice 12, 39-40, 90
  charity
    affinity of with humility . 31-32
    preeminent virtue 31
    toward neighbor 60
  chastity, fruitful,
    at Bethlehem 65
  complaints 65
  confessing plainly 30-31
  confidence 45-46
  conscience
    examination of 93, 95, 96
  consolations 78-79, 111-112
  constancy (equanimity)
    . . . . 16, 47-48, 79
    most essential virtue 17
  conversion 11, 38-39, 114
  despair 46
  detachment from
    consolations 78
  discouragement 46
  disorderly appetites 76-77
  even disposition the most
    pleasing virtue in 47-48
  fear 45-46
    and hope 45-46, 112
  hope 45-46
  humiliation 15
  humility. See Humility.
  imperfections 12-13
  inconstancy 16-17, 48
  intention, purity of 47
  joy and happiness 59, 60
  knowledge of one's misery . . . 11
  love. See Love.
  mortification . . 14-15, 34, 47-48

Spiritual life (cont.)
  obedience
    . . . . . . 58-59, 61, 95, 117-118
  Passion of Christ in 14-15
  patience—the true virtue
    of Christians 30
  peace and tranquility 60
  penance, penitence . . 16, 18, 35,
    36, 37, 40, 45, 47, (Note 1) 49
  penitential practices, great . . . 90
  poverty. See Poverty.
  presumption 21, 46, 47
  pride 10, 33, 45-47
    most powerful temptation . . 20
    originated in "heaven" 22
    rejected by Christ 13-14
  reason in control 58-61, 78
  repentance. See penance.
  resentment 12
  restlessness 60
  sadness 60
  self-complacency 13
  self-control or "keeping the
    night watch" 57
  self-love 11
  self-renunciation 77
  sensuality 89-90, 91
  silence 65
  sobriety, spiritual 76-77
  spiritual reading . . . . (2 refs.) 13
  tepidity 12-13, 117
  virtues
    enjoyed in Heaven 112
    true and false 111-112
Symbols
  bee/honey—Word/Mary 85
  beehive—Virgin's womb . 55, 85
  bees, mystical—senses,
    faculties, soul 60, 85
  queen bee—Our Lord
    . . . . 60, 61, 65
  breasts—affections 114
  burning bush—hypostatic
    union 64

Symbols (cont.)

butter—human nature 64

clothing ceremony—
Incarnation 68

dew and fleece—hypostatic
union 74-75

ear, left—listens to worldly
things 97

ear, right—listens to
inspirations 97

fire and iron—
hypostatic union 73-74

germ of sun's ray—Holy Spirit
in Our Lady's womb 64

hills, eternal—Patriarchs,
saints, angels 63

honey
divine nature 64, 85
holy and loving thoughts . . . 61
Incarnation 84-85

honey from thyme—
Jesus' humanity 84-85

horses—disorderly appetites . . 76

knife of circumcision—good
resolution 93

little lamb—our love 59

lizards—tepidity 12

manna
Eucharist 69-70
Incarnation 54-56, 69-70
tastes of, three:
bread (flour)—Our Lord's
body 55-56, 70
honey—divinity 55, 70
oil—Our Lord's soul
. . . . 55, 70-71

milk and honey 85

mountains—pride 45

myrrh—strength 114

polar star—Bl. V. Mary 53

rod of Moses—prodigies
of grace 116

sea and sponge—hypostatic
union 75-76

Symbols (cont.)

serpent biting its tail—
Divinity as Beginning
and End of all things 105

sheep—our spiritual flock
. . . . 56, 58

shepherds—bishops, superiors,
priests, spir. directors,
persons seeking
perfection 56-57

starlight—virgin birth 53, 54

sun and its rays—eternal
generation 84

swaddling clothes—obedience
. . . . 57-58

valleys
fear and discouragement
. . . . 45-46
tepidity 45

vesting of a prince—
Incarnation 68-69

water/wine—tepidity,
repentance/love 117

ways and roads—intentions . . . 47

worms—remorse of
conscience 40

Thais, St. 46

Theodosius, Emperor
. . . . 18, (note 12) 19

Thomas Aquinas, St.
on knowledge of our faith . . . 67

Time
belongs to God 87
consecrated to Our Lord 88
dedicated to gods 87-88
dedicated to saints 88

Trinity—
a Christian mystery 71

Urias 44

Vocation and election 37

Will of God, foreseen
conditioned by our prayers
. . . . 114-115

Word of God

Word of God (cont.)
    for the individual 37
        proclamation 37
    interior of Our Lord
        for creation 116
    in Holy Eucharist 116
        miracle at Cana 116
    obligation to listen to 13, 38
    obstacles to profiting by:
        procrastination 38-39

Word of God (cont.)
    obstacles to profiting by: (cont.)
        spiritual avarice 39
    spoken through Sts. John
        and Paul 36
Works
    criteria of a Christian 11
    testify who we are
        10-11, 18, 29, 46-47, 100-101
Zoroaster 106

Index to the Scriptural References

Gen. 1:26-27 106
    2:7 106
    3:1 22
    3:5 21
    3:9, 13 3
    3:12 4
    3:13 3
    3:15 10
    3:19 11
    17:10-14 . . . . .11, 88
    18:27 11
    25:21 114
    33:18-20; 34 97
    34 .97
    34:3 98
    47:9 41
    49:10 63
    49:26 . . . . 25, 63
Ex. 3:2 64
    3:14-15 100
    4:2-4 116
    7:19-20 116
    12:11 82
    16:6-7 . . . . .50, 51
    16:13-14 . . . . .53, 70
    16:16 39
    16:19-20 39
    16:21 . . . . 38, 53
    16:31 . . . . .53, 55, 70

    17:5-6 116
Lev. 12:3 88
Num. 11:7-9 . . . . .53, 70
    11:8 . . . . .55, 70
    11:9 52
    24:17 53
Deut. 18:15, 18 . . . . 28, 36
Jgs. 6:36-40 74
    11; 12 101
1 Kgs. (1 Sam.) 1:15 99
                1:18 60
                2:7-8 33
                7:3 64
                13:14 43
2 Kgs. (2 Sam.) 11; 12:1-14 . . .43
                12:13 . . . . . 4, 47
                22:14 10
Job 8:9 41
    14:2 41
Ps. 6:7 113
    21 (22):7 14
    34 (35):10 21
    38 (39):13 113
    39 (40):7-9 77
    41 (42):4 . . . . 44, 113
    44 (45):15 65
    49:13, 21 76
    50 (51):3 45
    54 (55):23 118

Ps. 55 (56):2 45
 55 (56):9 113
 61 (62):9 99
 63 (64):4 90
 77 (78):23-25 56
 77 (78):25 70
 96 (97):7 65
 101 (102):12 41
 103 (104):29-30 13
 112 (113):5 21
 112 (113):6-7 33
 112 (113):7 33
 3:1-3, 5-6 36
 3:2 37
 3:4 32
 3:5-6 36
 3:11 32
 3:13-17 2
 4:17 37
 5:19 92
 6:9-13 111
 6:34 39
 9:14 . . . . 7, 16, 36
 9:36 42
 11:2-10 1
 11:3 1
 11:10 . . . . 28, 33
 11:14 27
 19:17 91
 23:2 40
 23:12 . . . . 33, 46
 23:25-26 115
 26:51-52 97
 1:4-5 36
 2:18 . . . . 7, 16
 118 (119):164 83
 137 (138):6 33
 138 (139):1-9 3
 143 (144):4 41
 144 (145):19 77
Cant. 1:1 (1:2) 26
 1:2 (3) 55, 102
 1:3 (4) 55, 80
 1:6 (7) 65

Cant. 1:12 (13) 64, 114
Cant. 2:16 65
 3:11 107
 6.2 65
 7:2 (3) 65
 8:1 64
Wis. 1.5 13
 7:3 . . . . 58, 106
 16:20 . . . . .56, 70 (2 refs.)
 16:20, 25 54
 16:27-28 53
 16:28 38
 18:14-15 53
Ecclus. (Sir.) 7:40 (36) 83
    42:18-20 3
Is. 1:3 76
 7:14 53
 7:15 64
 14:13-14 21
 14:14 24
 33:7 5
 40:1-4 40
 40:3 31
 40:18 21
 42:8 100
 53:4-5 77
 61:1 13
 66:24 40
Lam. 2:19 99
Agg. 2:8 . . . . 25, 63
Mal. 3:1 33
 4:5 (3:23) 27
Matt. 1:16 100
 1:21 99
 2:1-2 104
 2:1-11 85
Mk. 7:3-6 115
 9:45, 47 (48) 40
 16:1 4
Lk. 1:6 12
 1:15 32
 1:17 27
 1:17, 76 37
 1:26-28 70

Lk. 1:35 . . . . 53, 84
　　1:41, 44 2
　　1:48, 52 33
　　1:52 . . . . 33, 46
　　1:55 85
　　1:76 . . . . . (2 refs.) 28, 33, 37
　　1:78 . . . . 43, 53
　　2:8 57
　　2:8-12 56
　　2:8-14 85
　　2:10-14 5
　　2:12 51
　　2:21 . . . . 87, 88
　　2:20 59
　　2:48 65
　　3:1-2 40
　　3:1-6 40
　　3:2 37
　　3:2-3 35
　　3:3 . . . . 32, 36
　　4:18 13
　　7:19 1
　　7:26, 28 . . . . 28, 33
　　11:2-4 77
　　12:35-40 . . . . . . (Note 1) 111
　　14:11 33
　　18:10-14 46
　　18:14 . . . . 33, 46
　　21:28 46
　　22:42 111
　　22:49-51 97
　　24:15, 17, 25-27 4
Jn. 1:5, 9 52
　　1:19 17
　　1:19-20 20
　　1:19-21 23
　　1:19-23 36
　　1:22-23 31
　　1:23 6
　　1:25 29
　　1:26 32
　　1:29 7
　　1:29-36 2
　　2:1-11 103

Jn. 3:16 68
　　6:31-32 70
　　6:33, 41, 50-51, 58 56
　　6:38 77
　　6:50, 52 (51), 55, 59 56
　　6:55 (54) 56
　　10:11, 14 57
　　10:27 61
　　18:10-11 97
　　19:28-29 75
　　20:11-15 4
Acts 2:17, 39 82
　　4:12 . . . . (2 refs.) 100
　　8:3 43
　　9:1 43
　　9:3-7 43
　　17:23 71
Rom. 1:3 85
　　1:21 71
　　2:4-5 47
　　8:29 85
　　9:33 14
　　13:11 46
1 Cor. 1:23 14
　　1:27-28 14
　　3:1-2 8
　　4:9-16 6
　　9:19-22 8
　　9:22 13
　　10:4, 11 116
　　10:16 107
　　11:24-27 107
　　13:8 30
　　15:9 43
2 Cor. 4:10 15
　　5:20 36
Gal. 1:13 43
　　3:16 85
　　4:19 . . . . 6, 8
Eph. 4:17-18 71
Phil. 2:6-7 80
　　2:7 84
　　2:9-10 102
　　4:5 45

Col. 1:15-18 85
    2:3 59
1 Thess. 2:7-8 8
    2:13 36
1 Tim. 6:16 54
    6:18 89
Heb. 1:3 89
    1:6 65
    2:9 80
    2:11-17 85
    2:17 59
    4:13 . . . . .3, 5
    4:15 84
    9:22 99
    10:5-9 77

Heb. 13:16 89
Jas. 2:10 92
    4:13-15 38
1 Ptr. 1:19 . . . . 72, 88
    2:7-8 14
    2:9 100
    1 Ptr. 5:4 56
    5:7 118
    5:8 61
2 Ptr. 1:4 84
1 Jn. 1:5 52
Apoc. (Rev.) 1:8 105
    5:12 72
    12:9 24
    22:13 105

If you have enjoyed this book, consider making your next selection from among the following . . .

The Facts About Luther. Msgr. Patrick O'Hare.................... 8.00
Little Catechism of the Curé of Ars. St. John Vianney............. 4.00
The Curé of Ars—Patron Saint of Parish Priests. Fr. B. O'Brien...... 3.50
Saint Teresa of Ávila. William Thomas Walsh.....................16.50
Isabella of Spain: The Last Crusader. William Thomas Walsh........16.50
Characters of the Inquisition. William Thomas Walsh...............10.00
Blood-Drenched Altars—Cath. Comment. on Hist. Mexico. Kelley....16.50
The Four Last Things—Death, Judgment, Hell, Heaven. Fr. Von Cochem 4.50
Confession of a Roman Catholic. Paul Whitcomb.................. 1.25
The Catholic Church Has the Answer. Paul Whitcomb.............. 1.25
The Sinner's Guide. Ven. Louis of Granada...................... 8.00
True Devotion to Mary. St. Louis De Montfort.................... 5.00
Life of St. Anthony Mary Claret. Fanchón Royer.................. 8.00
Autobiography of St. Anthony Mary Claret...................... 8.00
I Wait for You. Sr. Josefa Menendez............................ .50
Words of Love. Menendez, Betrone, Mary of the Trinity............ 3.00
Little Lives of the Great Saints. John O'Kane Murray..............12.00
Prayer—The Key to Salvation. Fr. Michael Müller................. 5.00
Sermons on Prayer. St. Francis de Sales........................ 3.00
Sermons on Our Lady. St. Francis de Sales...................... 7.00
Sermons for Lent. St. Francis de Sales......................... 8.00
Passion of Jesus and Its Hidden Meaning. Fr. Groenings, S.J..........9.00
The Victories of the Martyrs. St. Alphonsus Liguori............... 5.00
Canons and Decrees of the Council of Trent. Schroeder........... 8.00
Sermons of St. Alphonsus Liguori for Every Sunday...............10.00
A Catechism of Modernism. Fr. J. B. Lemius.................... 3.00
Alexandrina—The Agony and the Glory. Johnston.................. 2.50
Blessed Margaret of Castello. Fr. William Bonniwell.............. 4.00
The Ways of Mental Prayer. Dom Vitalis Lehodey................. 8.00
Fr. Paul of Moll. van Speybrouck............................. 6.00
St. Francis of Paola. Simi and Segreti......................... 4.50
Communion Under Both Kinds. Michael Davies................... 1.00
Abortion: Yes or No? Dr. John L. Grady, M.D................... 1.00
The Story of the Church. Johnson, Hannan, Dominica.............12.50
Religious Liberty. Michael Davies............................. 1.00
Hell Quizzes. Radio Replies Press............................. .60
Indulgence Quizzes. Radio Replies Press........................ .60
Purgatory Quizzes. Radio Replies Press......................... .60
Virgin and Statue Worship Quizzes. Radio Replies Press........... .60
The Holy Eucharist. St. Alphonsus............................ 5.00
Meditation Prayer on Mary Immaculate. Padre Pio................ .75
Little Book of the Work of Infinite Love. de la Touche............. 1.50
Textual Concordance of The Holy Scriptures.....................30.00
Douay-Rheims Bible. Leatherbound............................35.00
The Way of Divine Love. Sister Josefa Menendez.................12.00
The Way of Divine Love. (pocket, unabr.). Menendez.............. 5.00
Mystical City of God—Abridged. Ven. Mary of Agreda.............15.00

Prices guaranteed through December 31, 1988.

Raised from the Dead. Fr. Hebert.........................12.00
Love and Service of God, Infinite Love. Mother Louise Margaret..8.00
Life and Work of Mother Louise Margaret. Fr. O'Connell........8.00
Autobiography of St. Margaret Mary......................... 3.00
Thoughts and Sayings of St. Margaret Mary................... 2.50
The Voice of the Saints. Comp. by Francis Johnston........... 4.00
The 12 Steps to Holiness and Salvation. St. Alphonsus.......... 6.00
The Rosary and the Crisis of Faith. Cirrincione & Nelson....... .75
Sin and Its Consequences. Cardinal Manning................. 5.00
Fourfold Sovereignty of God. Cardinal Manning............... 4.50
Catholic Apologetics Today. Fr. Most...................... 6.00
Dialogue of St. Catherine of Siena. Transl. Algar Thorold....... 6.00
Catholic Answer to Jehovah's Witnesses. D'Angelo............. 5.50
Twelve Promises of the Sacred Heart. (100 cards)............. 4.00
St. Aloysius Gonzaga. Fr. Meschler....................... 7.00
The Love of Mary. D. Roberto............................ 5.00
Begone Satan. Fr. Vogl................................. 1.50
The Prophets and Our Times. Fr. R. G. Culleton............. 6.00
St. Therese, The Little Flower. John Beevers................. 3.50
St. Joseph of Copertino. Fr. Angelo Pastrovicchi.............. 3.00
Mary, The Second Eve. Cardinal Newman................... 1.50
Devotion to Infant Jesus of Prague. Booklet................... .40
The Faith of Our Fathers. Cardinal Gibbons.................. 9.00
The Wonder of Guadalupe. Francis Johnston................. 5.00
Apologetics. Msgr. Paul Glenn........................... 6.00
Baltimore Catechism No. 1............................... 2.00
Baltimore Catechism No. 2............................... 3.00
Baltimore Catechism No. 3............................... 5.00
An Explanation of the Baltimore Catechism. Fr. Kinkead....... 8.50
Bethlehem. Fr. Faber...................................10.00
Bible History. Schuster................................. 8.00
Blessed Eucharist. Fr. Mueller........................... 9.00
Catholic Catechism. Fr. Faerber.......................... 3.00
The Devil. Fr. Delaporte................................ 4.00
Dogmatic Theology for the Laity. Fr. Premm.................12.50
Evidence of Satan in the Modern World. Cristiani............. 5.50
Fifteen Promises of Mary. (100 cards)...................... 4.00
Life of Anne Catherine Emmerich. 2 vols. Schmoger...........33.00
Life of the Blessed Virgin Mary. Emmerich..................10.00
Manual of Practical Devotion to St. Joseph. Patrignani.......... 9.00
Prayer to St. Michael. (100 leaflets)....................... 4.00
Prayerbook of Favorite Litanies. Fr. Hebert.................. 7.50
Preparation for Death. (Abridged). St. Alphonsus.............. 5.00
Purgatory Explained. Schouppe........................... 8.50
Purgatory Explained. (pocket, unabr.). Schouppe.............. 5.00
Fundamentals of Catholic Dogma. Ludwig Ott................15.00
Spiritual Conferences. Tauler............................ 7.00
Trustful Surrender to Divine Providence. Bl. Claude........... 3.00
Wife, Mother and Mystic. Bessieres........................ 5.50
The Agony of Jesus. Padre Pio........................... 1.00

Prices guaranteed through December 31, 1988.

The Two Divine Promises. Fr. Hoppe...................... 1.00
Eucharistic Miracles. Joan Carroll Cruz.....................10.00
The Incorruptibles. Joan Carroll Cruz....................... 8.00
Birth Prevention Quizzes. Radio Replies Press................. .60
Pope St. Pius X. F. A. Forbes............................. 4.50
St. Alphonsus Liguori. Frs. Miller and Aubin.................12.50
Self-Abandonment to Divine Providence. Fr. de Caussade, S.J....12.50
The Song of Songs—A Mystical Exposition. Fr. Arintero, O.P....15.00
Prophecy for Today. Edward Connor........................ 3.00
A Year with the Saints. Anonymous........................ 5.00
Saint Michael and the Angels. Approved Sources.............. 3.50
Dolorous Passion of Our Lord. Anne C. Emmerich............10.00
Modern Saints—Their Lives & Faces. Ann Ball...............10.00
Our Lady of Fatima's Peace Plan from Heaven. Booklet......... .40
Divine Favors Granted to St. Joseph. Pere Binet.............. 3.00
St. Joseph Cafasso—Priest of the Gallows. St. J. Bosco......... 2.00
Catechism of the Council of Trent. McHugh/Callan............15.00
The Foot of the Cross. Fr. Faber...........................10.00
The Rosary in Action. John Johnson........................ 5.00
Padre Pio—The Stigmatist. Fr. Charles Carty................. 8.50
Why Squander Illness? Frs. Rumble & Carty.................. 1.50
The Sacred Heart and the Priesthood. de la Touche............ 5.00
Fatima—The Great Sign. Francis Johnston.................... 6.00
Heliotropium—Conformity of Human Will to Divine............ 8.50
Charity for the Suffering Souls. Fr. John Nageleisen............10.00
Devotion to the Sacred Heart of Jesus. Verheylezoon............ 8.50
Who Is Padre Pio? Radio Replies Press...................... 1.00
Child's Bible History. Knecht............................... 2.00
The Stigmata and Modern Science. Fr. Charles Carty........... .75
The Life of Christ. 4 Vols. H.B. Anne C. Emmerich..........67.00
St. Anthony—The Wonder Worker of Padua. Stoddard........... 2.50
The Precious Blood. Fr. Faber............................. 7.50
The Holy Shroud & Four Visions. Fr. O'Connell.............. 1.50
Clean Love in Courtship. Fr. Lawrence Lovasik................ 1.50
The Prophecies of St. Malachy. Peter Bander.................. 3.00
St. Martin de Porres. Giuliana Cavallini...................... 7.00
The Secret of the Rosary. St. Louis De Montfort.............. 1.00
The History of Antichrist. Rev. P. Huchede.................. 2.00
The Douay-Rheims New Testament. Paperbound............... 8.00
St. Catherine of Siena. Alice Curtayne...................... 7.50
Where We Got the Bible. Fr. Henry Graham.................. 3.00
Hidden Treasure—Holy Mass. St. Leonard.................... 2.50
Imitation of the Sacred Heart of Jesus. Fr. Arnoudt............10.00
The Life & Glories of St. Joseph. Edward Thompson........... 9.00
Père Lamy. Biver.. 6.00
Humility of Heart. Fr. Cajetan da Bergamo.................. 4.50
The Curé D'Ars. Abbé Francis Trochu.......................15.00
Love, Peace and Joy. St. Gertrude/Prévot.................... 4.00
Three Ways of the Spiritual Life. Garrigou-Lagrange.............3.00

At your bookdealer or direct from the publisher.

Prices guaranteed through December 31, 1988.